Teaching
Choral Music
A COURSE OF STUDY

MUSIC EDUCATORS NATIONAL CONFERENCE

Developed by the MENC Task Force on Choral Music Course of Study

Charles Hoffer, National Executive Board Liaison

Leon Burton, Chair
Marianne Holland
Doris Sjolund
Lynn Sjolund
Elizabeth Tabor

Contents

The MENC Task Force on Choral Music Course of Study has compiled *Teaching Choral Music: A Course of Study* to provide teachers with assistance in developing courses of study. In compiling this material, the Task Force members drew not only on their own training and experience but on that of music educators from across the country.

Rather than a complete or final recommended course of study, this document provides a representative approach that teachers can use in conjunction with the MENC publication *The School Music Program: Description and Standards* to improve the quality of music instruction at all levels. No endorsement of any particular method for music teaching is intended or should be inferred.

Foreword

There is a growing concern in public school education for each discipline to identify learning outcomes appropriate for the ages of children being taught. As a result of this general educational concern, music teachers are being asked to design courses of study in the same manner as teachers in other disciplines. It is reasonable that music educators be held accountable for what is being taught in classrooms and rehearsal halls. It is also reasonable to assume that students can demonstrate what they have learned as a consequence of the instruction delivered.

Teachers often contact MENC for assistance in developing courses of study for local school districts. In the spring of 1988 a meeting was held in conjunction with MENC's National Biennial In-Service Conference in Indiana to explore the development of courses in general music, band, orchestra, and chorus. It was agreed that MENC should proceed in generating such courses of study that could serve as models for any school district in the country. These courses would identify a sequence of outcomes for various ages and/or ability levels of music students.

Teachers with proven records of teaching success were selected to participate in each of the four projects. These educators spent more than two years developing materials simple and concise enough to be helpful for teachers as they plan instruction. Because each instructional area is unique, each committee was free to develop any format it felt appropriate. The four documents were never intended to be a "national" course of study; instead they offer teachers a model for the development of sequenced learning outcomes that meet their local needs.

The documents also reflect input from numerous other outstanding educators who took time to read rough drafts and respond to questionnaires. MENC hopes that teachers will find this document and the other three in the series helpful in administering sequenced music instruction that results in easily measurable learning outcomes.

Donald L. Corbett
Past President, MENC

Preface

An important question introspective music teachers ask themselves at different times in their professional careers is, What is appropriate content for the courses I teach and what attendant skills should I expect students to develop? Preservice courses at the tertiary level address some of the concerns implied by this question; state and district curriculum guides and course outlines offer some direction; and textbooks, particularly at the elementary level, usually include chronologies for presenting musical content and developing skills.

Introspective music teachers continue to search for answers because they want to achieve higher levels of comprehensiveness in school music programs and in the courses they teach. This ongoing yearning to refine and improve courses is the lifeblood of quality education. Should the yearning ever end, educational programs will stagnate.

Introduction

This course of study should serve as a body of information and recommendations that teachers and leaders in music education can draw on for designing and developing, rethinking and redesigning, or expanding and embellishing courses in vocal and choral music. The course of study is not a curriculum—a detailed, day-by-day account of every aspect involved in teaching vocal and choral music—rather, it contains *basic sets* of information and recommendations for grades 4–12 that pertain to the larger picture of vocal and choral music with implications for program expansion and improvement.

Information and recommendations are provided as helps for teachers and music program designers. This material relates to

■ children's choirs,

■ middle and junior high school choirs,

■ high school choirs,

■ the choral warm-up,

■ preparation for presenting music for study and performance,

■ the kind of repertoire believed to be appropriate for school choral programs,

■ vocal skills and choral techniques that need to be developed in grades 4–12,

■ the core choir and the value of supporting ensemble experience,

■ other aspects of choral music programs,

■ a conceptual framework for designing a sequential approach to musical understanding,

■ suggestions for evaluating the total vocal and choral program,

■ a glossary of musical terms relating specifically to choral music, and

■ a bibliography.

Of special help to teachers are the prototype lessons, which include a range of repertoire appropriate for school choral programs. Lessons for nineteen quality selections are provided as suggested models for a sequential approach to the study of choral music in classroom settings. A purpose of the model lessons is to suggest ways to work toward excellence in vocal production and choral performance while focusing on the development of musical understanding and aesthetic awareness and response.

This course of study has been conceived as a supplement to two publications of the Music Educators National Conference, *The School Music Program: Description and Standards* and *Guidelines for Performances of School Music Groups: Expectations and Limitations*. This new publication addresses in more specific detail the various elements of a school choral music program and presents recommendations for ensuring quality choral experience for singers.

It is envisioned that this course of study will be expanded and further refined in the future and become an even more practical resource for teachers and leaders in vocal and choral music. The Music Educators National Conference will be especially appreciative if users will keep notes on ideas for improving subsequent editions and make the notes available to the director of publications.

Curricular, Extra-Curricular, and Quasi-Curricular Choral Opportunities

A core choir (mixed, treble, or male) is recommended as the primary choral offering for school music programs. Participation in a core choir is vital to maintaining a balanced and effective program of choral music. It should also be a prerequisite for participation in satellite ensembles, and all ensembles should evolve from core choir experience.

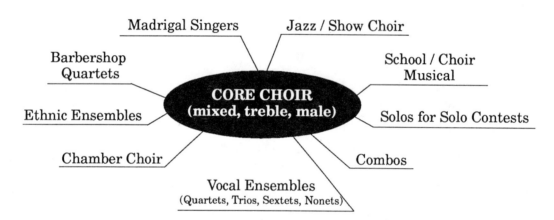

All ensembles, whether curricular, extra-curricular, or quasi-curricular, evolve from participation in the school's core choir.

Mixed chorus (with and without accompaniment), treble choirs, changed and unchanged voice choirs, male choirs, combos, small ensembles (duet, trio, quartet, sextet, show, jazz, pop), madrigals, chamber choir, ethnic choir, and barbershop ensembles each provide valuable musical opportunities and experience for singers. Some of the ensembles, however, are more appropriate for higher grades, and others may not be practical for all school choral programs.

Ensemble experience presented through a curricular, extra-curricular, or quasi-curricular approach or organization in the school will have great value for singers and for the school music program, but the total program needs to be conceived within a realistic set of priorities that lead to quality vocal and choral development. Excellence in any school music program is realized only when quality repertoire is presented in a way that guides the sequential development of vocal production, musical understanding, and artistic performance. Although community service functions provide good experience for singers, the goals of the school choral music program should receive first priority.

Repertoire

It is generally believed that the repertoire for a vocal and choral music program for grades 4–12 should include music of different historical periods, music of different styles, and music of different cultures. This belief is not expressed to suggest that each of the three categories be assigned one-third of the total instructional time, or that music of other cultures, for instance, constitute one-third of the total number of selections studied during a school year. Each teacher needs to determine a balance of the three categories that is appropriate for students in the program of a given school.

All repertoire selected for school programs should be of the highest possible quality. Good literature, carefully prepared and taught, is the basis for solid musical growth in the school program. These criteria for selecting repertoire are presented as reminders to help keep the goal of quality in the forefront. The repertoire selected should

- have musical qualities that are lasting, regardless of the level of difficulty;

- have discernible expressive content and positive textual appropriateness;

- have direct relationship to the school's objectives for the choral program;

- provide a balanced diet of musical styles, cultures, and historical periods during the students' involvement in the choral program;

- ensure experiences for students that are essential to successful performance and significant learning;

- be consistent with a vocal and choral skill development plan that gradually leads students into higher degrees of refinement;

- be appropriate for the age and experience levels of students;

- be appropriate in relation to available rehearsal and study time;

- have the potential for maintaining teacher and student interest;

- have accompaniment requirements that do not exceed available resources;

- have appropriate voicings and tessitura and realistic melodic, rhythmic, and harmonic requirements; and

- suggest relationships to other quality selections that can provide interesting rehearsal strategies and good programming ideas.

Participation in reading sessions of choral music is recommended as a significant way for teachers to become familiar with a wide range of repertoire and to sharpen their abilities to recognize quality selections. Visiting music stores, obtaining review copies from publishers, consulting with experienced colleagues, attending concerts performed by other school groups, and other means of reviewing and hearing new or unfamiliar repertoire will also be helpful. Participation in conferences and workshops of professional organizations is also highly recommended as a means of finding good choral literature.

Considerations for Preparing Music for Study and Performance

The following sixteen considerations are important when preparing choral music for study and performance. These considerations are not equally important to all selections, but each has some significance that will relate to study and performance goals. Although you will have additional musical problems to solve from time to time, this list is provided as a basic set to stimulate thought about the musical features of selections and their appropriateness for the students you teach.

- Tempos and tempo markings
- Meter and meter changes
- Notation and musical signs and symbols
- Key and key changes
- Voice ranges
- Entrances, cutoffs
- Movement of inner voices
- Dynamic levels and changes
- Beginning pitches of parts (initial pitches, as well as those after interludes or long rests)
- Length of introduction
- Length of interludes
- Phrase and harmonic analysis
- Implied mood
- Understanding of text (translation, if necessary)
- Language: diction, enunciation, pronunciation
- Style (period, background information on and intent of the composer)

Vocal Skills and Choral Techniques

There are many vocal skills and choral techniques that singers of all ages need to develop to continue reaching higher levels of musical maturity. It is essential that certain skills and techniques be introduced very early and then reinforced frequently over an extended period of time to ensure sequential development. Singers need to be shown individually how to focus their development in specific ways to ensure improvement.

The list that follows includes some of the more important skills and techniques that need to be introduced and refined. Other skills and techniques that will help to solve some of the problems singers encounter at various stages in their development should be added to this list by the choral conductor. Many books and articles by professionals in vocal and choral music address specific skills and techniques. These are good resources for conductors who need help in isolating some of the problems and working toward positive solutions. The Bibliography includes some resources that will be helpful.

Teachers are encouraged to plan for appropriate occasions during rehearsals to present examples from the repertoire being studied that will help to isolate skills and techniques for emphasis. Singers need to recognize how the development of skills and techniques relates directly to the music they are studying and to their long-range success as singers. Conductors are encouraged to expand this list and to keep it available as a reminder of areas that singers need to develop.

- Breathing (breath support)
- Tone quality
- Posture (sitting, standing)
- Diction (vowels, consonants, diphthongs, pronunciation, enunciation, articulation)
- Vibrato
- Blend and balance (listening to self and others, and to parts and their functions)
- Interpretation (growth and decay, style, understanding, and application)
- Intonation
- Sight singing
- Recognition of vocal problems
- Attack and release

The Choral Warm-Up

Vocal and physical warm-ups are important in the development of individual voices and choruses. The better individual chorus members sing, the better the chorus will sound. The ability to sing—like the skills necessary to play an instrument—can be developed in groups, and positive results can be achieved in moderately short periods of time.

As a general guide, approximately 20 percent of rehearsal time should be spent on vocal preparation. Sometimes it will be possible to use more time; at other times a brief warm-up may suffice. Most choral directors find that good choirs *want* the opportunity to do vocal exercises before rehearsing choral literature.

The choral warm-up should include physical exercises in addition to the vocal exercises. Stretching; relieving tensions in the shoulders, head and neck; aligning the body with the spine; and keeping the chest high prepare the body for singing. This physical preparation should lead to correct posture and an alert mental attitude prior to beginning vocal warm-ups and should continue throughout the rehearsal.

Here are some important points to consider for the use of vocalises and warm-ups that could help your choir improve:

■ Be sure you and your singers know what you desire to achieve with each warm-up. Vocal warm-ups should serve a specific purpose, and singers should always be aware of that purpose.

■ Begin with exercises that have limited, easy ranges and reasonable dynamic requirements.

■ Identify and isolate specific vocal problems (such as breath support, resonance and breathiness, flexibility and facility, extension of range, vowel uniformity, control of dynamics, achieving a "head voice," diction and enunciation, blend and uniformity of sound, balance, posture, freedom from tension, relaxed jaw and open mouth, intonation and pitch, precision and rhythmic clarity), and use exercises that will help eliminate those problems.

■ Use exercises with tuned consonants (*m, n, v, z*) on the attacks. These will help in tone placement and prevent the glottal shock often heard in young singers.

■ Use vocalises that will gradually extend pitch and dynamic ranges, particularly if it is early in the day or if the group has not been involved in singing for a period of time.

■ Provide constant encouragement for young singers and listen closely for signs of forcing or tension. Whenever strain or forcing appears, determine the reason for the problem and adjust or change the exercise.

■ Begin exercises in a comfortable singing range for your singers, and use descending patterns. Gradually raise the pitch by half steps, while maintaining the same quality of sound. Descending exercises help to eliminate "breaks" in the voice when careful attention is given; they also assist in developing the head voice. Ascending scale patterns and other ascending exercises may cause problems in vocal production if used before students have a good concept of sound in the upper ranges of the voice.

■ Vary vocal exercises. Repeated use of a single exercise may result in loss of effectiveness.

- Use exercises that allow all singers to sing easily in their vocal ranges. For choirs with changing and insecure voices, unison exercises are effective. Two-part, three-part, or four-part exercises are appropriate and effective in choirs with more developed voices.
- Design or compose your own exercises to assist in teaching a difficult part of a composition or to isolate special vocal problems.

Vocal exercises need not be limited to the beginning of rehearsals. They are also helpful in resolving specific problems within the selected repertoire being rehearsed.

Some Suggested Vocalises

1. The following vocalises will help to improve placement, breath support, resonance, and freedom.

use a) *oo*   b) *oh*   c) *ah*   d) some staccato, some legato

Noh ————— ah,   noh ————— ah,   noh ————— ah, etc.

Have students
- stand with hand on stomach and inhale against the hand.
- sing slowly and phonate through the *n* to the *oh* sound, keeping a slight tension against the hand; continue through the phrase while keeping the tension.
- retain the same buzz in the tone (resonance) as they move to the *oh* from the *n* sound.
- move gradually from the *oh* to the final *ah* sound so the tone keeps the same quality.
- release any tension in the jaw, keep the shoulders relaxed, and keep the chest high in order to have plenty of space for air.
- listen to determine if the same vowel is being formed by all singers. Use a word reference example such as *o* as in home or as in *no,* going to an *ah* as in father.
- roll shoulders forward or back, shake or roll the head, bend forward like rag dolls to eliminate tension.

2. This exercise is designed to teach students breath support and awareness of deep body involvement (diaphragmatic breathing). It should also teach students to plan for the use of breath control so they can sing a complete phrase.

s   s   s   s   sh sh sh sh   f   f   f   f   pt!

Have students
- stand.
- place their hands on sides, just under the rib cage.
- speak the sounds using one breath.
- use a moderate tempo with separation between each sound.
- become aware of increased resistance in the diaphragm throughout the exercise.
- exhale all the remaining breath on the last *pt,* and use the three counts of rest to replenish the air supply without moving the shoulders.

3. This exercise is designed to teach students resonance, sustained vowel line, and rapid articulation.

Min - nee mah - nee moh - nee, min - nee mah - nee moh - nee,

min - nee mah - nee moh - nee, min - nee mah - nee moh - nee

(continue in similar fashion down the C major scale
or any other major scale)

Have students
- ■ sing through the *m* sound and keep the hum in the vowel.
- ■ gradually increase the tempo until it can be sung with one breath and with one beat to a measure.
- ■ use a five-tone pattern if an entire scale is difficult to negotiate.
- ■ do the exercise as a canon with each voice entering two measures after the one before.
- ■ imagine the motion as moving up instead of down. Lifting a hand while descending will usually help intensity and pitch.

4. This exercise is designed to improve blend, balance, resonance, intonation, and chromatic movement.

* repeat this measure three times

Have students
- ■ start from the bottom of the chord and build as notated.
- ■ connect the *oh* and *ah* vowels carefully, avoiding *No-wah*.
- ■ see that each *ah* vowel blends with that sung by each of the other sections; keep the brightness in the *ah* (as in *fa*ther). For a darker sound, suggest an *aw* (as in law).
- ■ move the pitches up and down chromatically in the rhythm shown when the *ah* is in tune in all parts; the pattern should help students sing more accurately and with vitality in long phrases. It should also teach awareness of other parts.

5. Make up exercises to solve tonal and other vowel musical problems.
   Have students
   - ■ sing "America" in one breath for breath extension and to develop awareness of the necessity to plan for and conserve breath.
   - ■ sing a phrase on vowels *without* any consonants for awareness of vowel purity.
   - ■ count as far as they can on one breath.
   - ■ make siren sounds from their highest to lowest notes without forcing or changing quality.
   - ■ use a phrase of a song in various rhythms or in different ranges, ending with the written notes and rhythm.
   - ■ use a different phrase or section of the literature being studied.

Children's Choirs

Children's choirs provide unique opportunities for children to develop individual vocal skills and receive rich musical and aesthetic experiences. Since singing is only a part of the elementary school general music program, opportunities should be provided for children who wish to sing and receive a quality choral experience.

Young singers can develop good vocal skills when development is approached sequentially. By the end of the second grade, most singers should have developed confidence in unison singing. By the end of the third grade, they are ready to add ostinatos and eventually participate in two-part and three-part round singing. Echo songs are particularly useful at this level. Adding independent lines to melodies (such as a descant) and singing partner songs in grades three and four will help students develop independence in part singing. Singers can begin singing two-part choral arrangements by the fifth grade if choral development has been approached sequentially.

Vocal Modeling

While superior voice quality is not essential for any choral conductor, it is especially important that the conductor sing well enough to serve as a model for groups. Children are able to hear subtle differences and will learn to discern degrees of excellence quickly. They are also able to imitate subtleties and will try to please the conductor. It is possible to model diction, phrasing, tone quality, accents, and nuances as well as correct notes.

Repertoire

Young singers need to be introduced to music of different historical periods, styles, and cultures. Music stores, the choral libraries of colleagues in nearby schools, basic song texts, and many other sources are available for locating repertoire suitable for a particular group of children. Publishers, when requested, will often send sample copies for examination. A wealth of beautiful rounds and canons are available to those who will look for them. When searching for compositions of sufficient quality for your choir, you should establish a file card system that includes the title of a piece, voicing, composer, arranger, publisher and the publisher's code for the piece, and specific musical features that you may want to recall at a later time. This will bring real benefits as you select pieces for study and performance.

Membership

Elementary school choirs should be as inclusive as possible, recognizing that recommended grade or age levels of children will differ with each situation. A group of forty to eighty members in two grade levels works well. In a K–6 school, children in grades 5 and 6 are likely candidates. Since children in grade 4 generally have had less musical experience than children in grades 5 and 6, their participation could discourage older children. In a K–5 school, children in grades 4 and 5 can be grouped together successfully. When auditions are necessary, children should be asked to sing a short, well-known solo unaccompanied and to echo several patterns containing different intervals.

Scheduling

Scheduling rehearsals for the children's choir will generally require some delicate planning involving the school administration and parents. Rehearsals during the school day are best, but it may be necessary to rehearse during recess, lunch time, after school, or at other times. Ask for help! Involvement by the school principal, music coordinator, colleagues within the school who are sympathetic to the music program, and parents will help to establish a workable plan. To begin, two well-planned, thirty-minute rehearsals each week are adequate. Stressing the need for commitment by the children and their parents at the outset is important to the success of the first choral experience. Attendance and punctuality should be presented as requirements for participation.

Budgeting

Budgeting for children's choirs may prove to be a challenge. It is therefore important that financial needs be included in the decision to organize a children's choir as a part of the school's music program. These needs should be made known to school administrators, parents, and the librarian. It is valuable to note from the experiences of other music groups and teachers how funds for such a program are often provided from school discretionary funds and parents' organizations.

Rehearsals

The first rehearsal of the children's choir is very important. The rehearsal room should be arranged appropriately and should be ready prior to the rehearsal time. Folders (three-ring binders work well) and pencils should be available. The rehearsal order should be posted and explained. Vocalises that assist in good tone production and focus on individual listening should be included. Using overhead transparencies with examples of rhythmic or melodic patterns or writing examples on the chalkboard will contribute to the teaching of music reading. Each rehearsal should be a learning and musical experience. Young singers are as capable of producing good musical results as older singers.

Performances

When the choir can perform at least two musical selections reasonably well, schedule a mini-performance. Invite the principal, a custodian, a teacher friend, and others to listen to a rehearsal. Make an audiotape recording of the choir and a videotape recording, if possible. Have choir members critique their performance. Schedule a performance of the two songs for the student body, residents of a retirement home, or another group. A full-length program is not always desirable, or necessary, to maintain the interest of the children.

Rehearsal Guidelines

The following are some techniques and language proven to be useful in working with children's choirs. The goal should be to use descriptive directions during rehearsals rather than give comments that do not explain how to make improvements.

Instead of saying...	Use descriptive directions such as...
Use good posture.	Sit as if you were going to zip up your jacket.
	Stand as if you are ready to dive. Breathe deeply, and slowly lower your arms. Now you are ready to sing.
Take a good breath.	Breathe as if you had twenty noses around your belt. (You might even sketch a picture of this.)
	Take a breath from your big toe.
Sing with better tone.	Use your head voice while singing these scales downward.
	Let's sing with the vowel sounds we are trying to improve. (Use a familiar song.)
Use better diction.	Open your mouths. Doesn't that make an amazing difference? Take a bite out of a large imaginary apple and then begin singing.
	Let me read your lips. (Look at each singer to see if you really can read their lips.)
Put some life in that tone.	Sing with "big eyes."
	Sing as if it's a matter of life and death.
	Put all the forte sounds in a smaller package to sing piano.
Look at your music.	Find the color-coded green part at letter B. (Highlight the choral parts for beginners; put an X in the front of the staff they should follow.)
	Begin at letter B or measure 25. (This procedure will get students to look at the music.)
Phrase better.	Listen and sing this phrase exactly as I do.
	I'll sing two examples. You decide which example is more musical.
Sing with expression.	Listen to what this section sounds like with no expression. (Sometimes negative modeling can make a point.)
Follow the dynamics.	(Be specific.) At letter A there is a forte sign. You will need to sing one degree louder.
	You have been singing on step five of the dynamic ladder. At letter A you need to sing at step seven to create the forte indicated.

Junior High and Middle School Choirs

The middle school or junior high school chorus offers special challenges. Working to develop the good vocal habits discussed earlier is essential, even when you are faced with problems such as daily voice changes, singers' peer pressures, finding good choral literature for the age level, and schedules that may not permit a continuing choral experience at higher grade levels. There are as many problems as there are schools, and many of the problems must be addressed individually as they occur. When they do occur, seek assistance from colleagues, supervisors, MENC leaders, or leaders of American Choral Directors Association (ACDA). Do not hesitate to ask for help.

Repertoire

The problem of repertoire for this level is not insurmountable; it can be resolved by diligent searching. Music stores, conference displays, workshops, and colleagues' libraries all provide opportunities to examine unfamiliar music. Be prepared to arrange and rearrange music. Adapt selections for your singers' needs. You may need to change the key, change octaves, switch parts, and make other adjustments. Include selections with musical substance along with those that have instant appeal. Often, the melodic lines of Renaissance or Baroque music lead singers to discover beautiful choral sounds. Challenge your students. A challenge may be found in a canon or unison piece with limited range or in a selection with more parts. If a choral director does not introduce quality literature in the middle or junior high school, singers may not have another opportunity to experience it.

Get excited about your choices of music! Enthusiasm can be contagious. Do some research on the historical period; study and sing every vocal line yourself before introducing a piece. Examine the music for performance difficulties and the concepts that can be taught. Know the music thoroughly before presenting it to your singers.

Changing Voices

It is very important that students with changing voices feel successful both individually and as members of the choir. Guide them in learning to recognize their own voice changes so they can advise you of the new range difficulties they experience. You should assess each singer's vocal development periodically to prevent abuse of the changing voice, because students who are comfortable with singing will continue to sing. When needed, special parts should be written to fit the ranges of changing voices. For example, you may need to change selected notes in the tenor, baritone, or alto parts. Give attention to the changing female voice also. Girls should not continue to sing soprano or alto when the vocal range prevents them from doing so easily. It is most important that you establish conditions that prevent singers from becoming embarrassed or from considering the difficulties they experience as being insurmountable. Studying research concerning problems that singers have with changing voices will help you establish a positive educational climate for middle and junior high school choirs. Many studies of changing voices have been made and are available in books and periodicals.

Listening

Middle and junior high school students need to develop listening skills. They should sing unaccompanied often. In addition to listening to themselves by such methods as singing into a tape recorder or holding cupped hands over the ears, they should learn to listen to other sections, to their own section, to recordings, and to live performances. Guide them in learning what to listen for and how to become their own best critics.

Motivation

Achieving energetic singing is an important part of teaching in the middle and junior high school. This can be achieved in several different ways, including teacher modeling, using "tricks" to create facial expressions, giving constant reminders that singing takes energy, and complimenting good sounds and the way they were produced. Reverse modeling (singing without energy) will often appeal to this age level. Demonstrate how to sing with energy and without energy. Then ask, "Which kind of sound would your agent like to hear?" Help them decide. Keep your expectations high! The middle or junior high school choir can achieve surprising levels of musical performance if continually motivated.

Scheduling

It is important in the middle and junior high school to provide those who influence scheduling with detailed explanations about what is required to ensure a successful choral program. Exploratory music classes may offer varied musical opportunities for many students, but the continuity of the choral music program demands more than exploration. It is far more valuable to have a choir meet all year twice a week than to have it meet daily for one quarter. If limited to short-term groups, keep records of the students who should be recommended for continuing choral experience.

The ideal for beginners is to practice in single-sex groups. Experienced teachers agree that separating boys and girls develops students' confidence much faster and prevents negative reactions from the opposite sex. These groups could meet on alternate days (for example, on a schedule alternating physical education and music) and could be combined for performances. Mixed groups are more successful after individual and group confidence has been increased.

Performances

Plan with a supervisor, a colleague, or an administrator about how best to schedule activities for your choir. The junior high and middle school choir should not attempt to match the heavy performance schedule of some high school choirs. The feeling of success during a performance, however, creates a pleasurable and positive feeling for young singers. Plan mini-performances. Singers at this level love to perform and enjoy going anywhere. Attendance at rehearsals of other choirs, concerts, festivals, and other musical events without having to compete are valuable learning experiences for young singers. Ask a clinician to work with your singers. Learn to appreciate their highs and understand their lows. The rewards are great!

Further information about performances may be found in the MENC publication *Guidelines for Performances of School Music Groups: Expectations and Limitations.*

Aspects of the Choral Music Program

There are many different aspects of choral music programs that need to be woven into the day-to-day instructional process or to be presented as related, noninstructional activities that support the individual development of musical understandings, behaviors, and skills. The list that follows is a mixed set—a listing of a wide range of aspects that should be included in a choral music program with varying degrees of emphasis. Each teacher will need to determine the degree of prominence, space, or time that each of these and any other aspects will receive.

Some level of emphasis should be given to each area listed to ensure that every singer receives not only a balanced choral experience but also a balanced music education. A good choral experience should contribute to each student's becoming a skilled singer; a balanced musical experience should contribute to each student's becoming a musically educated person. The two areas complement each other.

An ideal way to present the many related aspects is to weave as many as possible into the daily instructional process and to devise ways all others could be embraced individually by singers to serve as supportive activities of the choral program. Add to this list other subjects that should become a part of the choral program and refer to it frequently as decisions are made about the content of courses and as daily teaching plans are developed or reconceptualized.

- Deportment and concert etiquette
- Private study
- Festivals
- Clinics
- Honors choral groups
- Community choral groups
- Attendance at concerts performed by others
- Viewing selected educational television programs
- Score reading
- Note reading, sight singing
- Analysis (music, text)
- Interpretation
- Researching
- Listening (ensemble rehearsal skill, recorded music)

- Ear training
- Accompanying
- Creativity (composing, arranging, improvising, harmonizing, accompanying melodies, chanting)
- Critiquing and evaluating
- Conducting
- Rote teaching and learning
- Styles (authentic, stylistic characteristics of historical periods)
- Leadership skills
- Care and use of instructional materials, music, and equipment
- Choreography (when appropriate)

Music Concept Framework

A Music Concept Framework is believed to be essential to an organized program of music instruction in which the purpose is to develop musical understanding. The concepts included in this framework are presented as a *basic set* that provides an example of sequential organization—simple to complex, concrete to more abstract. Teachers may, of course, find it necessary to delete some of the concepts listed, to add others, or to present some at higher or lower grade levels when there will be greater relevance to the repertoire being studied, the musical maturity of singers, or appropriateness for vocal and choral skill development.

The concepts listed represent some of the things that can be heard and understood through experience with vocal and choral music. Efforts to verbalize definitions of the concepts will be of value to singers only within a musical sound context. Conceptual understanding should be developed through the performance of vocal and choral repertoire. The prototype lessons presented later will provide some suggestions for developing musical understanding through rehearsals and other activities. A principal goal is to guide singers in understanding the music they are performing and to develop a bank of concepts from which they can draw in understanding other music they hear or perform.

The grade clusters used in organizing this framework are consistent with the publication *The School Music Program: Description and Standards.*

Concept	Grades 4–6	Grades 6–8/7–9	Grades 9–12
Tone			
pitch	x	o	o
loudness	x	o	o
timbre	x	o	o
duration	x	o	o
vibration		x	o
vibrato	x (recognized)	x (develop when appropriate)	o
Rhythm			
beat (pulse)	x	o	o
tempo	x	o	o
rhythm pattern (melodic/ nonmelodic, harmonic)	x	o	o
accent	x	o	o
meter	x	o	o
accelerando	x	o	o
ritardando	x	o	o
simple meter	x	o	o

Note: x = introduced   o = reinforced

Concept	Grades 4–6	Grades 6–8/7–9	Grades 9–12
Rhythm (*continued*)			
compound meter	x	o	o
thesis (downbeat)	x	o	o
anacrusis (upbeat)	x	o	o
syncopation	x	o	o
diminution		x	o
augmentation		x	o
composite meter			x
multimeter			x
Harmony			
simultaneous tones	x	o	o
consonance	x	o	o
dissonance	x	o	o
chord		x	o
chord progression		x	o
tonic chord		x	o
chord root		x	o
triad		x	o
non-chord tones		x	o
cluster			x
Tonality			
tonic	x	o	o
pentatonic	x	o	o
scale	x	o	o
major	x	o	o
minor	x	o	o
key signature		x	o
modulation		x	o
transposition		x	o
diatonic			x
chromatic			x
Texture			
accompaniment	x	o	o
unison	x	o	o
ostinato	x	o	o
round	x	o	o
partner songs	x	o	o
monophony	x	o	o
homophony	x	o	o
polyphony	x	o	o
canon	x	o	o
descant	x	o	o
solo	x	o	o
duet	x	o	o
trio	x	o	o
countermelody		x	o
antiphony		x	o
imitation		x	o
fugue			x
hocket			x

Concept	Grades 4–6	Grades 6–8/7–9	Grades 9–12
Form			
introduction	x	o	o
phrase	x	o	o
coda	x	o	o
interlude	x	o	o
contrast	x	o	o
recurrence	x	o	o
repetition	x	o	o
binary	x	o	o
ternary	x	o	o
operetta	x	o	o
opera	x	o	o
antiphony	x	o	o
canon	x	o	o
musical		x	o
mass			x
cantata			x
oratorio			x
theme			x
aria			x
motet			x
anthem			x
Melody			
call and response	x	o	o
speech-song	x	o	o
interval	x	o	o
legato	x	o	o
staccato	x	o	o
phrase	x	o	o
contour	x	o	o
sequence	x	o	o
range	x	o	o
arpeggio		x	o
blue notes			x
diatonic			x
chromatic			x
glissando			x
portamento			x
cadence			x
inversion			x

There are other concepts believed to be relevant to the study of music in a general way in grades 4–12. Some of the more prominent concepts considered to be appropriate to the study of music generally are counterpoint, heterophony, diatonic, concerto, section, rondo, program music, suite, theme and variations, overture, absolute music, twelve-bar blues, cyclical, period, sonata allegro, transposition, chant, conjunct/disjunct, key, atonality, circle of fifths, serialism, pitch class, orchestration, division of the beat, and hemiola. Such concepts should be embraced within a music program only as they relate to understanding the music being studied.

Prototype Lessons

Nineteen choral selections with suggested rehearsal strategies are presented as models that will serve as basic patterns for planning rehearsals. (A packet of printed music for the nineteen selections, *Choral Music Packet: Supplement to Teaching Choral Music*, is available from Music Educators National Conference.) The primary goals of the prototypes are to suggest ways attention may be focused on the development of musical understandings, vocal skills, and choral techniques during rehearsals; and to provide strategies that will be transferable to other choral selections. No attempt has been made to address all the vocal skills and choral techniques that might be possible for consideration for any one selection. It is assumed that the strategies you design for presenting choral selections will go beyond those provided in the prototypes.

The list of skills and techniques suggested for focus during rehearsals is presented again here as a reminder.

- Breathing (breath support)
- Tone quality
- Posture (sitting, standing)
- Diction (vowels, consonants, diphthongs, pronunciation, enunciation, articulation)
- Vibrato
- Blend and balance (listening to self and others and to parts and their functions)
- Interpretation (growth and decay, style, understanding, and application)
- Intonation
- Sight singing
- Recognition of vocal problems
- Attack and release

The selections included for the prototypes are representative of different styles, historical periods, and cultures. They also include a range of voicings from unison to SATB. Specific grade level designations have not been made because crossing grade levels is often necessary to accommodate various needs of choral groups. For instance, it may be appropriate in some situations to teach a unison piece to a mixed choir or a two-part piece to a high school boy's ensemble.

Each prototype includes some background information on the selection and its composer and/or arranger, a summary of the selection's salient musical features, a listing of musical terms (and in some instances signs and symbols) used by the composer, detailed rehearsal strategies, suggestions for the extension of musical understandings, and key evaluation questions for monitoring and assessing the progress of students.

Buttermilk Hill

(Song of 1776)
Ernst Bacon
SA, TB with Keyboard Accompaniment
Boosey and Hawkes #5944

Background

This two-part setting of a Revolutionary War tune was realized by Ernst Bacon, an American composer. Bacon provides an interesting accompaniment consisting of keyboard, a one-note violin part (which could be played by flute or recorder), a one-note bell part, and a part for small drum or tambourine. There are three verses, each accompanied by a different combination of instruments. The singers' notes remain the same in each verse and within the range of a tenth.

Musical Features

1. Legato lines in both parts.
2. Natural minor scale (or Aeolian mode).

Rehearsal Strategies

1. Have singers vocalize using *la* to *la*, a natural minor scale.

   With the scale written on the chalkboard, point to the syllables and have them sing the corresponding patterns you create. Include singing the interval from *la* down to *mi* and then to *do,* the beginning pitches of part 2.

2. Have all singers learn the melody. Insist on achieving a very legato line while maintaining vocal energy.
3. Show part 2 either on the chalkboard or overhead projector. Have all singers sing part 2 using syllables, numerals, or note names, listening for accuracy in the downward leaps.
4. Work to achieve a legato line by singing both parts on a neutral syllable such as *loo.*
5. Listen to the keyboard accompaniment played alone, then add the voice parts. Add the other instrumental parts later.

Musical Terms, Signs, and Symbols

Aeolian mode	dolce
intervals of fourths and fifths	legato
natural minor	slur

Extension

1. Sing the song in a detached, marcato style and listen for the change in mood.
2. Find and sing other songs in minor keys or modes (such as "Hey Ho, Nobody's Home," a round; or "Little Birch Tree," a Russian folk song).
3. Perform other songs from American colonial history (these might even be grouped as a section of a program).
4. Sing a round in both major and minor modes.

Evaluation

Can the singers

■ perform both parts with intervallic accuracy?

■ maintain intensity and vocal energy while performing at a soft dynamic level?

■ recognize a natural minor scale (Aeolian mode)?

Cantate Domino
Canticum Novum

(Sing a New Song to the Lord)
Richard Dering (edited by Susan Potter)
SAB
Presser Publishers #312-41270

Background

Composer Richard Dering (1590–1630) was a church musician in Belgium and England. He wrote this motet, No. 18 of 24 of the *Cantica Sacra,* for three voices and basso continuo. The keyboard part was realized by Susan Potter who also provided the English translation. The excellent foreword contains more information about the composer and the composition. This early Baroque composition uses ranges appropriate for any age group, although young baritones may need to sing the low A and G an octave higher to create a range within the C octave.

Musical Features

1. Meter changes between threes and twos ($\frac{3}{4}$ and $\frac{2}{2}$).
2. All parts perform rhythm patterns consisting of sixteenth notes.
3. Dynamics are terraced for contrast.
4. Harmonic progressions involve accidentals.

Rehearsal Strategies

1. The first sixteen bars in $\frac{3}{4}$ can be sung after each part has read the text in rhythm. The Latin text will allow for pure vowel production. Help the singers

discover that the baritone line is in contrary motion to the soprano and alto lines. After the three parts are sung separately, they should be sung together.

2. Discuss with the singers their ideas about the composer's intent when only one part sings to the Lord and then all three parts sing to the Lord. Does one part represent individuals singing to the Lord? Do all three parts together represent all people singing to the Lord?

3. Before singing the $\frac{2}{2}$ section (m. 18), prepare singers by displaying and practicing some of the rhythm patterns they will encounter.

Clap the rhythms or sing them on *doot* or *deet*, then add the text. Chant in rhythm before adding the pitches. On the chalkboard or an overhead transparency, mark the half note pulses and insist that singers show the pulses by tapping them on the thigh or in another observable way.

4. The individual parts in mm. 26–31 may need to be tapped, clapped, and sung in sectional rehearsals to obtain accuracy. Each part has its own rhythmic challenges. Each part also uses less rapid note values as it reaches the cadence, which produces a "measured ritard."

5. When returning to the $\frac{3}{4}$ meter for three measures (mm. 32–35), have the students conduct in one (or keep the pulse in one) to feel the same pulse in the $\frac{2}{2}$ section ($\downarrow . = \downarrow$). It will help to rehearse the rhythm alone, changing the subdivision from threes to twos.

6. The final twelve bars contain rhythmic passages that must be isolated and practiced. To be certain that the rhythms are accurate, use the quarter note as a pulse and gradually increase the tempo until the half-note pulse is comfortable. Then add the text and chant in rhythm, adding the pitches when the rhythms are secure.

7. As the pitches are added, note the accidentals. Stop at cadences to feel a key center; point out the reasons for the accidentals (such as C major to G major to A minor, and so on).

8. When performing the repeated section, ask the singers to continue to show the pulse through the meter changes.

9. Perform the entire piece with rhythmic vitality, listening for accuracy in intonation, matched vowel sounds, and weighted syllables. Since the tempo markings in this period are editorial, slow the tempo if the rhythmic vitality cannot be maintained in your choir.

Musical Terms, Signs, and Symbols

allegretto   basso continuo

changing meters between $\frac{3}{4}$ and $\frac{2}{2}$ forte

piano $\downarrow = 108$

Extension

1. Have a cellist or a bassoonist perform the bass line of the keyboard accompaniment.

2. Find other settings of the same text and perform them as a group for a concert.

3. Investigate the possibility of performing more motets from the *Cantica Sacra* or having small ensembles perform them. Complete the concert group with the full choir singing this motet.
4. Do a simple harmonic analysis of this piece.

Evaluation

Can the singers

■ maintain the pulse from one section to another?

■ accurately perform the rhythms?

■ demonstrate awareness of the terraced dynamics?

Coulters Candy

Arranged by Robert DeCormier
Two-part chorus for treble voices
G. Schirmer #51621

Background

This Scottish lullaby (Glasgow) for two-part chorus of treble voices with piano accompaniment has been arranged by one of America's folk song authorities. Robert DeCormier has chosen to begin and end this arrangement with a unison refrain that contains a syncopated rhythm suggesting the "Scottish snap." The Scottish charm of the text appeals to all ages, and the ranges are also appropriate for singers of all ages.

Musical Features

1. Syncopated rhythms and the Scottish snap ♪ ♩.are evident.
2. Melody line written in alto part.
3. Soprano harmony contains some divisi and is melodic in its own right.

Rehearsal Strategies

1. The entire chorus should learn the melody of the refrain and verse to experience the stylistic syncopated rhythms. Insist on a light, heady sound. The use of a chest voice should be discouraged since it will negatively affect the intended character of the lullaby.
2. All singers should learn part 1 of the repetitions of the refrain and note the slight changes in the middle repetition.
3. Sing through the piece with all singers performing in unison on the verses and in parts on the refrain. Continue to discourage use of the chest voice.
4. Have all singers learn part 1 of verse 1. Then perform verse 1 with two parts.
5. Have all singers read the soprano line of verse 2 and determine where and how it

differs from verse 1. Close attention to this difference in the early stages will aid accurate memorization later.
6. The opening phrases of verses 2 and 3 may be used as vocalises (on a neutral syllable). It will be most effective to display the notation for these phrases on the chalkboard, a chart, or an overhead transparency. Singers can then be challenged to find those lines on their scores.
7. Practice finding the beginning pitches following the introduction and the interludes.

Musical Terms, Signs, and Symbols

descant	Scottish snap
slur	syncopation

Extension

1. Have the chorus switch parts. Altos sing the descant and sopranos the melody. Analyze the change in character resulting from switching parts.
2. Prepare listening lessons or other songs that include the characteristic Scottish snap, such as Beethoven's *Schottische Lieder* and "Comin' Thro' the Rye."
3. Perform a group of lullabies from around the world and compare their musical content with that of "Coulters Candy."

Evaluation

Can the singers

■ perform the syncopated rhythms accurately?

■ use a head voice effectively?

■ sing harmony parts accurately without covering the melody?

■ recognize and sing the ♪ ♩. (Scottish snap) consistently?

Crawdad Hole

Mary Goetze, arranger
Three-part treble chorus
Boosey & Hawkes #6184

Background

This lively American folk song has been arranged by Mary Goetze, a well-known clinician and composer for children's choruses. The text has a "Huck Finn" appeal, and will delight both girls and boys as well as audiences.

Musical Features

1. Free rhythm, quasi-recitative style in vocal introduction.
2. Catchy rhythms that include sixteenth notes and dotted rhythms.
3. Melody accompanied by two repetitive countermelodies in outer voices.

Rehearsal Strategies

1. Use vocalises and warm-ups such as the following:
   a. Create recitatives using one pitch, thirds, or a variety of scale tones.
   b. Chant a nursery rhyme "a la recitative."
   c. Sing descending scales following a conductor's fermatas and ritards.
   d. Read, clap, or sizzle ("ss"), adding words to these rhythms:

from the melody   [rhythm notation]   "You get a line and I'll get a pole"

[rhythm notation]   "We'll go fishing in a crawdad hole."

from lower countermelody   [rhythm notation]   "my honey, my baby"

[rhythm notation]   "Get a pole and let's go fishing."

from upper countermelody   [rhythm notation]   "Hook, line, and sinker."

[rhythm notation]   "Yes, I have a hook."

2. Have all singers learn the melody using precise rhythms to create vitality. Have them identify the rhythms from the warm-ups as they occur in the melody.
3. Have all singers learn the lower countermelody (mm. 3–10); combine the countermelody with the melody.
4. Have all singers learn the upper countermelody (mm. 18–25). Then combine this countermelody with the melody.
5. Perform the two countermelodies and the melody together (mm. 27–34). Experiment singing at different dynamic levels until arriving at the desired balance levels.
6. Learn the introduction, the interludes, and the coda.

Musical Terms, Signs, and Symbols

allegretto	a tempo
breath mark	crescendo
countermelody	fermata
first and second endings	forte, piano, mezzo forte, mezzo piano
recitative style	ritard
slur	tie

Extension

1. Conduct a "treasure hunt" in other pieces; look for musical symbols and terms.
2. Use partner songs as warm-ups and out-of-class activities.

3. Sing other pieces that have countermelodies, such as "Who Killed Cock Robin?" arranged by Berteaux.
4. Listen to examples of recitative in cantatas and operas, such as Handel's *Messiah* or operas by Mozart.
5. Compare these countermelodies with the balanced melodic lines of the parts in a Renaissance piece.

Evaluation

Can the singers

■ read the notated rhythm patterns?

■ follow the conductor's ritards and fermatas?

■ sing at appropriate dynamic levels to achieve a desirable balance when the melody is in the middle voice?

David's Lamentation

William Billings, arranged by Elie Siegmeister
SATB
Carl Fischer Inc. #CM6572

Background

This piece was written by America's first professional composer, William Billings (1746–1800). His works are mostly hymn tunes or patriotic melodies that he wrote during the Revolutionary War. This text is biblical (David's sorrow over the death of his son Absalom), but the music is appropriate in public schools as a quality example of early American choral literature. The ranges are appropriate for any age, including eighth and ninth grade (tenors' tessitura is a fifth; basses' is an octave, and the lower octave could be changed to fit early stages of the changing voice).

Musical Features

1. Homophonic style requires ensemble phrasing.
2. When the text, "O, my son," is repeated, contrast in dynamics is indicated.
3. Sustained notes and long phrases occur in all parts.
4. Minor mode is used throughout.

Rehearsal Strategies

1. Sing minor scales or scale patterns legato, forte, and pianissimo in preparation for rehearsing the piece.
2. While singing the first eight bars, practice breathing (phrasing) together at the commas in the text (mm. 4, 6, 8). Observe the crescendos and decrescendos, which will lead to the natural rise and fall of each phrase. Have the students place breath marks or red lines in the places where they must breathe together.

3. Continue to sing the eight bars on a neutral syllable (*loo*) to create a very legato sound. Have two parts sing duets while the other singers listen to critique the performance for legato sound, intonation, and the rise and fall of phrase lines. For instance, sopranos and tenors can sing for the altos and basses. Encourage those who critique to listen for everything!

4. Continue rehearsing through mm. 14–18. The measures marked *p* must be sung with the intense feeling of the text, following the dramatic rest that Billings wrote.

5. The final ten bars must be phrased together. Have students mark phrases in mm. 21, 23, 26, and before the final "my son." The parts are quite easy, generally stepwise, so the singers can concentrate on matching vowels, dynamics, and phrasing. Singing on neutral syllables often will help to develop legato style.

Musical Terms, Signs, and Symbols

crescendo   decrescendo

marcato lines   pianissimo, piano, forte

triplet eighth-note pattern

Extension

1. Sing other songs by Billings. "Chester," "Easter Anthem," and "Rose of Sharon" are good examples.

2. Have a drama teacher or student read the text for the choir to note the use of facial expressions. Videotape the choir performing the piece and have them critique it for dramatic expression.

3. Program a group of songs by American composers or a group of songs written at the same period in other countries.

4. Have students research the lyrics on which the text is based.

Evaluation

Can the singers

■ sing uniform phrases, vowel sounds, and dynamics required for this slow, sustained piece?

■ perform the contrasting forte and piano phrases while maintaining intensity?

■ enunciate the text accurately?

Deshi

Brent Pierce
SA or TB
Plymouth Music Publishers #BP-500

Background

American composer Brent Pierce likens this piece to a "morning raga" and states that the raga "comes as close to emulating Indian music as Western music will allow." The prescribed pitches of the raga, on which the improvisation is based, are the notes of a natural c minor scale with a raised sixth. A three-bar repeated pattern of the piano introduction is the nucleus of the selection; the pattern is also characteristic of the Indian raga as it provides continuing support to a unison melody and descant. The haunting modal music and unusual rhythms of "Deshi" (a female name) will appeal to all ages.

Musical Features

1. Melody is in unusual mode—same as prescribed pitches of raga; could be compared with Western melodic minor scale, which is often altered by raised sixth.
2. Irregular rhythms punctuated with eighth and quarter rests create the unique character of unison melody and descant.
3. Middle section includes sixteenth notes in two-bar and four-bar ostinato that correspond to syllables of tabla (drum) player.
4. First three-measure phrase of piano introduction repeats and accompanies other melodies—a characteristic of the Indian raga.

Rehearsal Strategies

1. Sing a Western melodic minor scale using neutral syllables as a vocalise—raising the sixth degree of the scale—to prepare for this raga melody.
2. For variety, begin with the middle section. Practice the rhythm of the ostinato in part 2 (♩ ♩ ♫♫ ♩ | ♫ ♫ ♩ ♩). Speak the text in rhythm; it represents the syllables of the tabla player. Perform the ostinato as written, avoiding a heavy chest voice. Add the pitches of the ostinato.
3. Learn part 1, the melody above the ostinato. Perform the two parts together.
4. Practice the opening of the middle section with parts moving in contrary directions (p. 3). Study the repeated two-bar patterns that occur in both parts. Continue through the previously learned four-bar ostinato and melody (p. 4 to the top of p. 6).
5. Begin the A section by chanting the rhythm of the melody while keeping a regular beat, visually differentiating strong and weak beats. After the rhythms are secure, learn the melody. Sing it, and continue singing through the B section (both parts) and then the repeated A melody. Include the whispered "Deshi" and the final cadence with the accent and fermata.
6. Return to the beginning and sing the descant on a neutral syllable, concentrating on accurate pitches and rhythms. When the pitches are secure, add the text. Then add the melody to the descant.
7. Before singing the entire piece, listen to the repeated three-bar pattern of the piano introduction and note how many repetitions there are in the accompaniment (the nucleus of Indian raga). Add the vocal lines. Note that Pierce gives

dynamic levels to assist choruses in achieving appropriate balance between melody and accompanying vocal lines.
8. Consider singing the entire piece a whole step higher to accommodate the vocal experience and range of young or less experienced singers.

Musical Terms, Signs, and Symbols

accent	altered minor
dynamics	eighth, quarter, half rests
fermata	natural minor
ostinato	raga
sixteenth notes	tabla

Extension

1. Add wind chimes, finger cymbals, woodblocks, or conga drum for authentic effects.
2. Find out more about Indian customs, geography, folk instruments, and musical history.
3. Listen to a recording of an authentic raga such as Ravi Shankar's performance on *Sounds of India* Columbia CL9296.
4. Another raga-like piece composed by Brent Pierce is "Mukari," published by Jenson. This piece includes some improvisation on a prescribed set of tones and would provide a good follow-up performance experience.
5. Sing a familiar song and then alter notes to match the prescribed pitches of this raga.
6. Use the well-developed materials and lessons in the publication *Multicultural Perspectives in Music Education* (Music Educators National Conference, 1989), Chapter 7: India.

Evaluation

Can the singers

■ sing accurately the modal raga melody?

■ observe the eighth, quarter, and half rests?

■ accurately perform sixteenth notes?

■ recognize the repeated patterns within this raga?

Duet from Cantata No. 15

(Laughing and Shouting for Joy)
Bach (edited by Doreen Rao)
SA, Keyboard
Boosey & Hawkes #OC2B6454

Background

The editor lists J. S. Bach as composer of this cantata. Norton lists Johann Ludwig Bach (1677–1730) as composer. In either case, this duet was originally written for solo voices but is both appropriate and accessible for a treble ensemble of any age. Both parts have strong melodic lines that allow young singers to feel secure while performing a polyphonic piece. English and German texts are provided. An instructional videotape titled *On Location with Doreen Rao and the Glen Ellyn Children's Chorus* is available through ACDA, P.O. Box 6310, Lawton, Oklahoma, 73506.

Musical Features

1. Subject outlines a triad; both parts sing subject, but on different triads.
2. Countersubject is a six-note descending chromatic passage; each part sings the passage, each starting on a different note.
3. B section mostly in unison, but with some thirds.
4. Word painting throughout; subject and countersubject relate to meaning of text.

Rehearsal Strategies

1. Begin with warm-ups based on triadic movement and singing of the chromatic scale.
2. Copy and display the subject with its triadic patterns as it appears in mm. 12–14 in the soprano part and in mm. 15–19 of the alto part. Have students sing the patterns. Point out that the alto melody is sung in a different key. Note how the music matches the joyous text. Encourage singers to achieve a joyous tone quality.
3. Copy and display the chromatically moving countermelody as it occurs in mm. 12–14 of the alto part and in mm. 15–17 of the soprano part. Have students sing both examples. Note that the soprano part is a fifth higher than the alto part. Point out to the singers how this music expresses the sorrow of the text; encourage them to express the same sorrow in their vocal quality.
4. The A section, mm. 12–22, consists of both melodies sung simultaneously. Sing the section, matching vocal quality to the texts.
5. The B section begins with altos (mm. 26–27) answered by sopranos and then a duet in thirds (mm. 30–33). Rehearse this carefully, observing the rests in the duet. Encourage singers to think the pitches of the musical lines during the rests.
6. Guide the singers to discover that the second half of the B section includes a soprano imitation that is a fourth higher (mm. 34–35) than the alto part in mm. 26–27, and an alto imitation in mm. 36–37 that is a fifth lower than the soprano answer in mm. 28–29. The imitations are followed by a duet that is higher than the previous duet.

7. The piece may conclude with either the instrumental coda or with a repetition of the A section to m. 25.

Musical Terms, Signs, and Symbols

ABA form

countersubject

imitation

thirds

word painting

chromatic scale

D.S. al Fine

subject

triadic movement

Extension

1. Other duets from Bach cantatas could be used to extend students' experience.
2. Follow-up listening lessons could include other works with a subject and countersubject, such as Bach's "Little Fugue in G Minor."
3. Examples of word painting can be found in other works, such as Handel's *Messiah*.
4. Have the students sing the selection using neutral syllables in the style of the Swingle Singers.
5. Try a simple harmonic analysis of this Bach duet.
6. Use a string quartet for an accompaniment instead of a keyboard instrument.

Evaluation

Can the singers

■ recognize and differentiate between the subject and countersubject?

■ describe how the texts relate to the music of the subject and the music of the countersubject?

■ identify the sections of the ABA form?

Keep Your Lamps

Andre Thomas
SATB
Hinshaw Publishing Co. #HMC-577

Background

This spiritual is arranged for SATB (a cappella) with parts for high, medium, and low conga drums. The text has two meanings: it refers to a biblical parable and to the Underground Railroad. Andre Thomas, an Afro-American composer, added the drums as a twentieth-century defiance of the earlier outlawing of drums that were considered a sign of African ancestry. The basically homophonic yet strongly rhythmic style could be sung satisfactorily by any age group.

Musical Features

1. Natural minor (f minor) scale used with occasional raised seventh.
2. Middle section contrasts by having three lower parts accompany soprano part with legato chords.
3. Syncopation occurs regularly over barline.
4. Male voice ranges appropriate for middle school or junior high mixed chorus with tenors singing between A and F, baritones B♭ to F, and limited ranges for soprano and alto.

Rehearsal Strategies

1. Post numbers and syllables from low *la* to high *do* (a tenth) on the chalkboard. Vocalize a major scale; point to the notes. Vocalize natural minor scales (*la* to *la*) and change from natural minor to harmonic minor by raising *sol* one half step. Sing a harmonic minor scale up and a natural minor scale down. The music follows this pattern with an exception in m. 31 of the alto part. Pay close attention to intonation of the altered note.
2. Ask all singers to speak in rhythm the words "trimmed and burning" while keeping a visible beat. This can be done with clapping, tapping, swaying, or other bodily movement. Note the tie that creates syncopation at the barline.
3. The range of the melody is a sixth. Ask all singers to sing the melody of the soprano part. Enjoy the feel of the raised note in the second phrase and contrast it with the other phrases. Snapping fingers on every after beat or touching the music on the beat will encourage ending words together and improve precision of the rhythm.
4. Before singing all four parts, have each section sing their first four notes on the "scale ladder," pointing to the notes on the board first, then the music. Avoid using the piano if at all possible. Sing the first eight measures like a slow, precise march with a heavy, plodding pulse.
5. Have all singers learn the soprano melody (mm. 24–32) and produce an intensifying and relaxing of each phrase within the dynamic marking, using the word "weary" as the center of each phrase.
6. Rehearse the alto, tenor, and bass accompaniment on page 4. Heed the dynamic markings; they give life to the legato tone and add variety and color to the soprano solo.
7. Note the first and second endings and fermatas. Rehearse the marcato section at m. 70 and practice the *fp* with the final nuance.

Musical Terms, Signs, and Symbols

accidentals	alla breve
crescendo	decrescendo
fermata	first and second endings
forte	fortepiano
harmonic minor	marcato
natural minor	natural sign
piano	ritard
slur	syncopation
tie	

Extension

1. Sing other well-known spirituals. Sing them in unison as warm-ups.
2. Look for other spirituals in minor keys and note any accidentals that occur.
3. Search for other spirituals that were used to communicate ideas about the Underground Railroad, such as "Follow the Drinkin' Gourd."
4. Use the spiritual as a unison processional, singing the accompaniment after the chorus is in place. The conga drums may be used for an introduction, interludes, or a coda for musical interest and to extend the piece.

Evaluation

Can the singers

■ sing raised notes and syncopations accurately?

■ achieve a heavy pulse in their singing?

■ perform the three lower parts accurately and produce a vital sound when accompanying the soprano solo?

■ perform the notated dynamics and expressions effectively to make the music come alive?

Let Sounds of Joy Be Heard

Robert Schumann/Pfautsch
TBB
Lawson-Gould Publishers #52090

Background

This energetic song for men's voices was originally set by Schumann (1810–1856) for three bass voices. It is a good first song for young men to sing together. The ranges are appropriate for young voices, and the rhythms are strong, yet uncomplicated. The technical problems are few, so singers can listen to the other parts as they sing. The music can be learned in a short period of time and can provide young men an opportunity to perform a composition by a recognized master.

Musical Features

1. Melody the same in all three parts.
2. Strong dissonance, but approached stepwise.
3. German text provided; could add authenticity to performance.

Rehearsal Strategies

1. Look at the music and find repetitions of the melody.
2. Use a vocalise that stresses listening to minor and major seconds in sequences.
3. Read the phrases in German. If you do not feel confident with the language, have a student studying German assist the singers. Always break phrases into short

segments for rehearsal and insist that singers repeat the phrases forcefully. Be sure every singer is involved in this process. Gradually extend phrase lengths as you repeat the words.

4. Sing the theme in unison on a neutral syllable. Then repeat it using the German lyrics.
5. Sing the entire selection as written but without dynamics and at a slower tempo. Be aware of chromatic movement and accidentals.
6. Review all the markings and then sing the entire song with special awareness of the gradual increase in dynamic intensity to the brief coda.

Musical Terms, Signs, and Symbols

accidental   chromatic

fermata   theme

Extension

1. Learn other songs by Schumann.
2. Play recordings of other examples of Schumann's choral music.
3. Have students learn about *Fasching,* its significance to German-speaking countries, and whether non–German-speaking countries have similar celebrations (such as Mardi Gras and carnival seasons).
4. Sing choruses by other German or Romantic composers that have themes of celebration.
5. Give examples of music used in celebrations in our own society.

Evaluation

Can the singers

■ sing their parts accurately?

■ pronounce the German text accurately and with energy?

■ recognize the strength and joy in the song and demonstrate it in their performance?

Lord, I Sing a Song of Joy

Dvořák/Hopson
Unison
Belwin Mills #DMC-8160

Background

The arrangement of this joyful anthem from Dvořák's *Biblical Songs,* Op.99, Volume 1, includes a simplified keyboard accompaniment. Originally conceived as a vocal solo, the voice parts of the arrangement range from low *sol* to high *sol.* This anthem is an example of late–nineteenth-century vocal literature and can be performed by singers of all ages.

Musical Features

1. Four short verses requiring precise diction and phrasing.
2. B section rich in contrasting dynamics and rhythms.
3. Wide dynamic range (from *pp* through *fff,* including crescendos, decrescendos, and accents).
4. Varying phrase lengths.

Rehearsal Strategies

1. For warm-ups, practice dynamic changes, crescendos, and decrescendos on unison notes or chords.
2. Have singers model a soloist (teacher or older student) and echo the three phrases of verse 1 with the same precise diction, breathing, and dynamics intended for a final performance.
3. Continue with the next two verses. Pay special attention to the dynamics, phrasing, and diction (especially the key words in each verse).
4. Learn the contrasting section. Notice the syncopated rhythm on which the section begins and the long, dotted half notes in the closing phrases. Maintain the energy in the tone as the dynamic level decreases.
5. Sing the entire piece noting the repetitive, but effective, piano introduction, interludes, and coda.

Musical Terms, Signs, and Symbols

a tempo	accent
anthem	coda
crescendo	decrescendo
interlude	pianissimo, mezzo piano, mezzo forte, forte, fortissimo
ritard	syncopation

Extension

1. Discuss what makes this anthem a representative example of the Romantic period.
2. Learn more of Dvořák's *Biblical Songs* or invite an artist singer to perform them for the choir.
3. Listen to Dvořák's "New World Symphony" for Romantic qualities similar to those of the anthem.

Evaluation

Can the singers

■ perform accurately all the dynamic level markings in the piece?

■ recognize the contrasts in the B section?

■ phrase together?

■ match vowel sounds and enunciate the consonants with precision?

O Music,
Thou Most Lovely Art

(Musik dein ganz lieblich Kunst)
Johann Jeep, edited by Ray Robinson
SATB
Hinshaw Music Inc. #HMC-934

Background

German organist and kapellmeister, Johann Jeep (pronounced "Yeep" in German), 1562–1650, wrote a number of secular songs. This selection includes the German text and the editor's English translation. Other editions of this selection are available and may be useful in making comparisons for accurate interpretation. Keyboard is intended for rehearsal purposes only. The early Baroque style is evident in independent lines, imitative entrances, and phrases that reach beyond the barlines. A sixteen-measure section is repeated with a different text.

Musical Features

1. Each part enters independently, imitating first and second themes at fifth or octave.
2. Phrases in each part extend across barlines.
3. Half-note triplets in final section.
4. Limited ranges and secular text in praise of music make piece useful for both young and older choirs.

Rehearsal Strategies

1. Sing the opening pattern as a vocal exercise using neutral syllables and then the German and English texts.

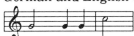

2. All parts should sing the first four bars of the soprano or tenor part. Pay special attention to singing it musically (for example, repeated notes and long notes should be performed with growing intensity and the final word of the phrase sung without accent). Be particular about clear consonants and pure vowels.
3. Sing the first eight measures noting that the soprano and alto have stepwise extensions following the motive. Weight the important English or German syllables of each part to obtain musical phrasing. Sing mm. 17–24, which repeat the music with a different text. Continue working on weighting important syllables and singing long and repeated notes with growing intensity while keeping a steady tempo.
4. Bars eight through twelve introduce a new musical idea. Rehearse the alto and tenor parts as a duet, then the bass and soprano lines as a duet. Put the four parts together. The upper parts finish the section (mm. 12–16) with stepwise lines. Again, weight the important syllables to achieve more intensity and avoid a stagnant vocal line. Mm. 23–32 repeat the notes of mm. 8–16 with a different text and a different inflection, which should be observed.
5. The slow, triplet chordal pattern (mm. 33–34) could be sung as a vocal exercise. Practice a legato, forte sound without distortion. The triplet pattern will be no problem for students *if* the conductor has carefully worked out how to direct this section (feel the whole note pulse and divide into threes).

6. A way to begin the final section is to isolate the bass line. All singers should sing it with numbers, syllables, note names, and neutral syllables. Then add the text, pointing out the important syllables. The other parts may then be added to that line to complete the piece. Retain the rise and fall of each phrase.

Musical Terms, Signs, and Symbols

accidentals	fifth
half-note triplets	imitation
motive	octave
phrase	

Extension

1. Have quartets or octets perform the piece for the chorus to enable other members to listen for arched phrases.
2. Perform another early Baroque piece and note how the line in each part is important and independent.
3. Program a group of songs with praise of music as the theme: "Musica est Dei," de Lassus (from *Canons on Music,* edited by Decker); or "Viva la Music," Praetorius, a three-part round. Music has often been the subject of songs throughout music history.

Evaluation

Can the singers

■ accurately sing imitative entrances?

■ shape the lines of their part as if each line were a solo?

■ feel the climax when singing the forte legato chords?

Rejoice in the Lord Alway

Anonymous (previously attributed to Redford)
SATB
Oxford University Press #43.243,
Tudor Church Music Series (TCM 55)

Background

This fine anthem was composed in the sixteenth century; the composer remains unknown. It was probably written during the same period that Byrd, Tallis, Gibbons, and Tye were composing. The anthem should be sung a cappella, but an organ reduction of the parts is given. It can be used to work on many of the features of Renaissance music without having to teach Latin pronunciation. Several different kinds of imitations and tone painting are used. Because the ranges are not extreme, it can be sung by any proficient group of singers with changed voices capable of singing a low B♭.

Musical Features

1. Imitation occurs in each part.
2. Imitation alternates with homophonic structure and is repeated for emphasis.
3. Movement of the music changes to fit text, such as in mm. 26–33.
4. Accented syllables give the piece variety and motion.

Rehearsal Strategies

1. Vocalize using easy descending patterns on *oo* and *oh* vowels to establish a pure head tone.
2. Use a vocalise that misplaces accents. For example: *1*234, 12*3*4, 123*4*, and 1234. Adapt these patterns to the words and show how the meaning changes (such as **RE**-joice in the Lord al-**WAY**, or re-**JOICE** in the Lord **AL**-way).
3. Look at the music and find where imitation occurs, how it occurs, and whether it occurs at the fifth, octave, two beats apart, or several measures apart, and so forth.
4. Sing the anthem starting with the easy sections that are homophonic, such as mm. 26–33 and mm. 39½–46. Then learn the a-men, showing how the lower parts enhance the single note held in the soprano.
5. Now sing the entire song. Try to avoid accenting the first beats of measures when unaccented syllables occur, but stress important syllables rather than strong beats. Point out that choral compositions of this period were written with few barlines.
6. The piece should move easily in a constant pulse that allows for changes in inflection. See that each part has a life of its own.

Musical Terms, Signs, and Symbols

agogic accents	anthem
homophony	imitation
polyphony	Renaissance

Extension

1. Compare this English anthem with those of Palestrina ("Alma Redemptoris Mater") or Victoria ("Ave Maria") to see similarities in style by other masters of this period from other countries.
2. Listen to a good recording of choruses singing music of this period.
3. Compare this anthem with secular music such as madrigals from the same period and country.
4. Perform the anthem for the chorus as a quartet so other singers can listen to gain understanding of the importance of each part.

Evaluation

Can the singers

■ sing their parts with proper accents?

■ produce a tone quality appropriate to the period and style?

■ show awareness of other contrasting parts as they sing their own?

■ discuss the Renaissance characteristics of this piece?

Ríu, Ríu, Chíu

Noah Greenberg, editor
*SATB (with baritone or bass solo and
percussion accompaniment)
Associated Music Publishers NYPM Series #10*

Background

This is the third of *Three Spanish Christmas Carols of the Sixteenth Century*. Noah Greenberg of New York ProMusica edited this ancient carol and wrote it a major second higher than the original version. The barlines between the staves are included only as a guide for the conductor and performer; the original version was written without barlines. Both Spanish and English texts are provided with a percussion line for tambourine or ad lib handclapping. The call-and-response form is typical of the popular music of this period. Each of the seven solo verses is answered by a repeated four-part chorus forming a modified call and response.

Musical Features

1. Music without barlines—sixteenth-century style of writing.
2. Second and third phrases have imitative entrances that use ideas from solo part.
3. All parts have limited range.
4. Constant shifts in accents give music character and vitality.
5. Accompaniment allows for variety of instrumental sounds.

Rehearsal Strategies

1. Clap the rhythm at a moderate tempo several times. Then gradually increase the tempo until the pulse is felt as a half note.
2. Look at the Spanish text and read it in rhythm. Pronunciation by a leader and response by the chorus is the most effective way to learn a foreign text. The leader must be well acquainted with the language and insist that the response be energetic and accurate.
3. Sing the scale on which the piece is based and determine which mode the scale represents. (Note that the mode is Dorian with half steps occuring between the second and third steps and the sixth and seventh steps of the scale.)
4. Singers should sing the melody with the text several times to feel the pulse and develop a sense of how they flow together.
5. Rehearse the parts on pages 2 and 3; insist on accuracy in pitch and rhythms; give special attention to the imitative entrances and the extension of phrases.
6. Combine all the parts and rehearse the piece following the suggestions of the editor and using one or more soloists on the verses.

Musical Terms, Signs, and Symbols

call-and-response form   dal segno sign
Dorian mode   imitation
tutti

Extension

1. Compare music of the troubadors and trouvères with this piece to identify similarities and differences.
2. Listen to recordings of the music of early composers such as Guillame de Machaut or Josquin de Pres to hear the freedom of expression within the regularity of pulse.
3. Find examples of songs using a similar structure in other periods of music history.
4. Find other selections that use modes other than major or minor.
5. Look through the text again to find changes in dynamic character.
6. All three of the Spanish carols could be performed on a program (with a Spanish dessert served afterwards!).

Evaluation

Can the singers

■ show evidence of feeling the rhythm of the song?

■ clap the rhythm and sing their parts accurately?

■ sing the response in such a way to match the character and energy of the solo?

■ determine whether the verses change in intensity and quality to match the expressive content of the text, such as verse 1 "raging mad," verse 4 "In sweet voices..."?

Sing We and Chant It

Thomas Morley, edited by Geoffrey Mason
SSATB
Walton Publishing Co. #7014-5

Background

A madrigal is a setting of secular verse that was popular in England at the end of the sixteenth and the beginning of the seventeenth century. It is an outgrowth of the earlier Italian madrigal, and Thomas Morley (1558–1602) was its guiding force. Morley wrote about one hundred such works and also acted as an editor and publisher for many other composers. This composition for five voices is typical of his writing. Though basically homophonic, rhythms and melodies play against each other in various combinations that generally express a carefree, joyous style.

Musical Features

1. Strongly tonal.
2. Characteristic madrigal style using contrasting dynamics.
3. Rhythmic diversity enhances parts and creates contrast.
4. First soprano part starts at a pitch lower than the second part, making ranges similar if not the same.

5. Text lends itself to easy addition of phrases using syllables *fa, la, la, la,* which is typical of madrigal style.

Rehearsal Strategies

1. Isolate rhythm patterns and clap or chant them together. Use examples such as those found in the first soprano part (mm. 5 and 6) or the second soprano part (mm. 6 and 7).
2. Note how the rhythms in the second soprano part (mm. 6–7) form a hemiola. To show the contrasts, have one part tap, clap, or chant *1* 2 3, *1* 2 3 while the other part does *1* 2, *1* 2, *1* 2.
3. Look for important words or syllables and show why they are stressed to make the song flow.
4. Have parts sing in pairs to show how each part has individual character and still fits with the other part.
5. Speak the words in rhythm emphasizing the absolute need for clarity of consonants as they might be pronounced by a British actor.
6. Have students conduct large circles in rhythm while singing or speaking the words in order to feel the flow of the music.
7. As the correct tempos are achieved, observe the tradition of repeating all parts at a contrasting dynamic level. The loud/soft pattern should be continued until the last few measures.

Musical Terms, Signs, and Symbols

hemiola   homophonic

madrigal   poco ritard

Extension

1. Listen to recordings of madrigals sung by English artists.
2. Find other Morley madrigals and perform them. Some well-known, accessible examples are "Now Is the Month of the Maying," "My Bonnie Lass She Smileth," and "Fire, Fire, My Heart."
3. Read materials about madrigals and the period from which they came.
4. When students have a good understanding of the genre, have them sing or listen to P.D.Q. Bach (Peter Schickele), "My Bonnie Lass She Smelleth" or "The Queen to Me a Royal Pain Doth Give."
5. Perform madrigals in Elizabethan costumes.
6. Present an Elizabethan dinner or festival.

Evaluation

Can the singers

■ perform all rhythms correctly?

■ sing the lyrics so they can be understood?

■ sing the *fa, la, la, la* sections in a crisp and light style?

■ perform dynamic contrasts without changes in intensity and quality?

■ maintain the individual character of each voice part to make them interesting to the listener and singer?

Six Folk Songs

Johannes Brahms
SATB
Marks Publishing, distributed by
Hal Leonard #00007913 MC9

Background

These songs are six of the twenty-six folk songs Brahms set for unaccompanied mixed chorus and are classic examples of fine choral literature. The piano reduction for rehearsals is by Herbert Zipper, the English translations by Harold Heiberg.

"I'd Enter Your Garden"	A tender love song.
"The Fiddler"	A lively song of a musical miracle.
"How Sad Flow the Streams"	A gentle, four-versed song about lovers parting.
"At Night"	A haunting selection about an evening rendezvous.
"Awake, Awake!"	A song of joy for the coming day and a plea to a loved one to rise and see the dawning; tenors have the melody for most of the third verse.
"A House Stands 'neath the Willow's Shade"	Three sparkling verses about two sweethearts.

Musical Features

"I'd Enter Your Garden"	Homophonic style allows for work on uniform vowels and tone quality; unified phrasing can be easily taught.
"The Fiddler"	Changing meters ($\frac{4}{4}$ to $\frac{5}{4}$); requires rapid enunciation and precise diction.
"How Sad Flow the Streams"	Beautiful tone quality essential for the text and musical line; phrases interrupted by rests must continue the vocal line.
"At Night"	Feeling of longing and unrest calls for rhythmic precision; dynamics change.
"Awake, Awake!"	Phrasing as a section and between parts important; primarily homophonic; phrase endings and beginnings vary to give character and variety.
"A House Stands 'neath the Willow's Shade"	Light, soft, staccato style (leggiero) used throughout; numerous accents call for precise diction and enhance staccato singing.

Rehearsal Strategies

(provided for "A House Stands 'neath the Willow's Shade" only)
1. Vocalize scale patterns with staccato articulations. Accent different notes within a vocalise while alternating between piano and forte (such as *1* 2 3 4, 1 *2* 3 4, 1 2 *3* 4, 1 2 3 *4*).
2. Speak the text of the first verse in rhythm. Have all singers speak each part, beginning with the bass part. Observe accents, staccato markings, and all dynamic markings while speaking in rhythm.
3. Exaggerate the consonants and the contrasts and be especially aware of precise final consonants and rests while speaking the text.
4. When singing the pitches, use a neutral syllable (*doot* on staccato notes and *doo* on legato notes). Continue to stress accents, dynamics, and style. When all is secure, add the text. The adding of words to the music should not change the leggiero style.
5. Treat the next two verses in the same careful way.
6. Discuss the importance of blend and balance for this piece.

Musical Terms, Signs, and Symbols

accent	changing meters
crescendo	dotted rhythm
forte	leggiero
piano	repeat sign
sixteenth notes	

Extension

1. Sing other musical works from the Romantic period by Schumann, Schubert, or Mendelssohn.
2. Perform the entire set of folk songs as a group to show contrasts in style and ability to be expressive within each style.
3. Perform other Brahms choral pieces that are not derived from folk songs.
4. Listen to recordings of Brahms' choral music, songs, short piano pieces, and chamber music.

Evaluation

(for "A House Stands..." only)

Can the singers

■ achieve a leggiero style?

■ use the accents and dynamic changes to enhance the musical performance?

■ use diction sufficiently clear for the casual listener to understand each word?

This We Know

Ron Jeffers
SATB
Earthsongs (220 NW 29th Street,
Corvallis, Oregon 97330) #52

Background

Ron Jeffers' contemporary setting of a text by Chief Seattle (1854) was first performed for the First World Symposium on Choral Music held in Vienna, Austria in 1987. The composer, a faculty member at Oregon State University, dedicated the piece to the International Federation for Choral Music and to the "abiding wisdom and spirit of Chief Seattle." Excellent performance notes are provided in the singers' scores.

Musical Features

1. Nature of the music suggests intense choral tone.
2. Unusual harmonic structure.
3. Range of dynamic contrasts and changing meters.
4. Varying phrase lengths.
5. Syllabic stress adds to expressive qualities.

Rehearsal Strategies

1. Read the text and performance notes to understand the composer's source of inspiration. The Indian phrase (vocables) "Teaah chlah usidwih" needs to be examined carefully by the teacher and then repeated by the singers until it is correct and fluent.
2. Rehearse until all four parts are accurate.
3. Be aware of all markings and musical terms. Singers should determine how and why each was selected and used to help express the ideas in the music.
4. Note the repetition of the phrase "This We Know." Have the chorus sing each of these phrases and explain how each repetition is different both in notation and in feeling.
5. Sing the song in phrases and notice that each syllable has a note of its own. Also, determine the number of syllables in each phrase. Ask singers to explain how the phrase lengths affect the feelings generated by the music.
6. Examine the text in relation to meters and accents on syllables. Sing the phrases with awareness of these accents. Perhaps the text should be spoken several times for students to become aware of syllabic weight.
7. To achieve the intensity desired, sing the piece at different dynamic levels. Suggest that as much energy be used to sing softly as to sing loudly. The soft sections must be projected with the intensity of a stage whisper.
8. When the phrases cannot be sung on one breath (mm. 12–17 and 21–25), plan where singers can stagger breathing so that a continuous band of sound is achieved. Experiment with different tempos. Singers will discover that a moderately slow tempo is appropriate when they sing the text and vocal lines.
9. Eventually the song must be sung as a single unit expressing the unity and interdependence of each part of the music as it moves to the final statement.

Musical Terms, Signs, and Symbols

crescendo	decrescendo
fermata	homophony
marcato	mezzo forte, piano, mezzo piano, pianissimo

Extension

1. Have the chorus members describe their feelings about the composition and use contemporary examples to show the relevance of the music to the present age.
2. Encourage the singers to share their understandings of the urgency of the composition's message and the solid strength of the music.
3. Ask the chorus to explain how the text and music have been welded into a single idea.

Evaluation

Can the singers

- ■ sing complete phrases with intense choral tone?

- ■ explain how the music and text are compatible?

- ■ discuss their own feelings about the piece?

- ■ understand the significance of the metric and dynamic changes?

Three Canons for Voice

Persichetti
Three-part for mixed voices
Presser Publishers #362-03268

Background

The three canons were written by Persichetti, one of America's leading contemporary composers. No. 1 "Should Fancy Cease" is based on words in Sanskrit, a sacred and learned Indian language. No. 2, "Preface to Canons," has a humorous text written by Reichenbach. He states "The primary element of a canon is not the score but the melody...it is deplorable if a piano is necessary for studying the tune." No. 3, "Halleluja, Bum Again," is a text from folklore. The first of the canons is sung as a tender, expressive melodic line; the second, a fast, rhythmic canon for two parts with extreme dynamic contrasts; the third, a boisterous rendition of a five-word text for two parts with an accompanying ostinato.

Because the canons were written for women's, men's, or mixed voices, they can be used by a chorus at any level of proficiency. The ranges are within a tenth, but changing voices could switch octaves to better fit their ranges.

Musical Features

1. All three canons have numerous contrasting dynamic and articulation markings.
2. Each canon has an expressive phrase line and contrasting phrase lines.
3. Each canon incorporates wide intervals (sixths, sevenths, octaves) as well as stepwise lines.
4. Each canon has special rhythmic features including rhythmic motives and changing meters ($\frac{3}{2}$ to $\frac{2}{2}$).
5. Aeolian mode used in the first canon, Dorian mode in the third.

Rehearsal Strategies

No. 1 "Should Fancy Cease"
1. Have singers of all parts mark a half-note pulse while singing. Be sure that the half-note continues to be the constant (regular) pulse when changing from a meter of threes to a meter of twos.
2. Work for precision in observing rests to avoid overlapping harmonies.
3. Stress the need to accurately perform the two wide intervals within the given dynamic markings.
4. Exaggerate the consonants while emphasizing the words "fancy," "world," and "dead." Add the second part only after the single line sounds precise and musical.
5. Add the third part after confidence is established with the first two parts.
6. The canon is repeated three times, each time softer. Keep the tempo and the intensity of sound moving to the end (a challenge because it is marked *ppp*).

No. 2 "Preface to Canons"
1. Since the canon is long (twenty-eight measures) and has rhythmic phrases of varying lengths, have the singers mark the quarter-note pulse and speak the words in rhythm. It is recommended that the canon be rehearsed by sentences.
2. Add crescendos, decrescendos, marcato, sostenuto to the rhythmic reading of the text.
3. A young choir could whisper words in rhythm while hearing the melody played, perhaps a two-measure phrase at a time. Sing the melody.
4. On another day, rehearse the last phrase (top of p. 5) as a vocalise for sostenuto singing while observing crescendos and decrescendos. The octave downward leap on the word "mastered" could be used as a vocal exercise for singing forte-legato and piano-staccato.
5. Finally, put the canon together, insisting that singers keep a steady beat.

No. 3 "Halleluja, Bum Again"
1. Vocalize on a Dorian scale, noting the half steps between scale tones two and three and six and seven.
2. Sing the final four notes of the canon as a vocal exercise, raising the pattern by half steps and practicing the crescendo ending with a jump of a seventh.
3. Sing the entire theme articulating ⁻ followed by >. After part 1 is accurate, have all singers read the one-pitch ostinato pattern, counting the rests in a stage whisper. Point out that this device is called a pedal point or drone.
4. Sing the ostinato with the dynamics indicated. Add it to part 1 and have the singers perform both parts.
5. Add part 2 at a later time; have singers switch parts to increase awareness of structure.

Musical Terms, Signs, and Symbols

accent	Aeolian mode
changing meters	crescendo
decrescendo	diminuendo
Dorian mode	marcato
pedal point (drone)	*ppp, pp, p, mp, mf, f, ff, fff*
poco a poco	ritardando
staccato	

Extension

1. Develop a repertoire of rounds by various composers and styles to acquaint singers with sounds of each of the periods of music history.
2. Listen to other music by Persichetti to identify similarities and differences with the three canons.
3. Sing a Persichetti two-part song such as "Sam Was a Man," "Hist Whist," or "Four Cummings Choruses."
4. Copy the melody of the first canon using different meters (changing $\frac{3}{2}$ to $\frac{6}{4}$ and $\frac{2}{2}$ to $\frac{4}{4}$). Discuss why a composer might select one meter rather than another.

Evaluation

Can the singers

■ demonstrate *all* the indicated dynamics and articulations?

■ listen to a recording of their performance and critique it using musical criteria?

■ recognize differences in the style of contrasting phrases?

■ accurately sing the intervals (sixths, sevenths, octaves)?

■ keep a constant pulse through the changing meters and rhythmic texts?

Vanitas Vanitatum

(Vanity, Vanity, All is Vanity)
Jan Sweelinck (edited by Doreen Rao)
Two-, three-, or four-part canon
Boosey & Hawkes #OCTB6351

Background

This six-bar, late Renaissance canon for two, three, or four parts is edited by Doreen Rao, a nationally known authority on children's chorus. The canon is in B♭ major and has a range of an eleventh. The secular text consists of four Latin words; a diction guide is provided by the editor. The canon includes dotted rhythms and a short melismatic fragment that together create an interesting melody and a beautiful canon. Both children and adults will enjoy singing this piece by Sweelinck (1562–1621). Changing voices might have some difficulty with the range, but the low *do* could be sung an octave higher making the range a ninth.

Musical Features

1. Beautiful six-bar melody.
2. Syllables of the Latin words weighted to produce appropriate phrasing (syllables underscored by the editor).
3. Open, pure vowel sounds of the Latin text.
4. Melismatic line characteristic of the Renaissance.

Rehearsal Strategies

1. Write the following rhythm patterns on the chalkboard or on poster paper. Have singers echo the patterns on *ss,* then sing them on a neutral syllable such as *moo.* Find the patterns in the canon; sing them with the syllables or scale tones of the melody.

2. Sing the entire melody on a neutral syllable such as *loo,* singing stresses where indicated.
3. Speak the Latin words using consonants to help stess the underscored syllables. Demonstrate and insist on open *ah* and *o* vowels. Sing the Latin text while maintaining a legato line and stressing the indicated syllables.
4. When the singers can perform the melody with correct musical expression, divide them into two parts and sing the piece as a canon. Retain the legato sound, the weighted syllables, and the open vowels. Continue in three parts, then four parts as the group gains confidence.

Musical Terms, Signs, and Symbols

canon	dotted quarter
fermata	melisma
Renaissance	repeat signs
sixteenth notes	tied eighth notes
weighted syllables	

Extension

1. Use other rounds and canons to begin rehearsals or to introduce your choir to part-singing. Try "Jubilate Deo" by Praetorius and edited by Rao, rounds from basic song textbooks, special books of rounds like *Old Rounds and New Canons* by Harry Robert Wilson and *101 Canons* and *Sacred Canons* published by World Around Songs.
2. Find another Renaissance piece and see what characteristics are the same or similar.
3. Find out more about the life and times of Sweelinck.
4. Compose a canon on a favorite phrase or proverb.
5. Add handbells. Transpose the piece to the key of C and play it on the recorder.

Evaluation

Can the singers

■ perform a legato line with weighted syllables?

■ hear and produce open vowel sounds?

■ recognize the melisma and perform it accurately?

■ explain what the musical features of a Renaissance canon are?

We Hasten, O Jesu

Bach/Davies
Two-part
Oxford University Press #A234

Background

This duet is from Bach's Cantata No. 78, "Jesu, der du meine Seele." The English text is provided by the arranger. The keyboard accompaniment is written for organ or piano but could be played effectively by a string quartet. This arrangement is appropriate for all ages. E. C. Schirmer (#2506) publishes the same duet with the B section as well, but the harmonies and general difficulty of the B section suggest it would be more appropriate for an advanced group. This arrangement is appropriate for all ages.

Musical Features

1. Word painting occurs throughout. "Hasten" demands fluency; "faltering" is sung with a melody that goes up and back but generally works its way up; "O, Master" is sung with a pleading inflection.
2. Imitation at the fifth occurs in entrances.
3. Each voice line is melodic within Bach's established harmony.
4. Melody requires use of head voice throughout; chest voice will not allow flexibility needed by second part, nor will it allow higher pitches to be sung with ease and strength.

Rehearsal Strategies

1. Listen to a performance of the piece, or have two skilled sopranos perform it to help singers become acquainted with its style.
2. Both parts begin with the same rhythmic and melodic pattern; have singers chant, clap, or sing the rhythm of the first four measures of part 2.
3. Have both parts sing the stepwise melody on a neutral syllable such as *doo*.
4. Add the text while maintaining rhythmic accuracy.
5. Have part 1 sing the first eight measures. Note how it is like part 2 (the opening four-measure melisma) and how it is different (a fourth higher). Rehearse the two parts together for the first ten measures.
6. The next ten measures contain the same rhythmic patterns. Rehearse these parts carefully; note that there are some changes in the melodic line.
7. The last section contains the same melismatic rhythmic patterns followed by a more homophonic section, first in sixths, and later in thirds. An optional ritornello (short instrumental section) provides a coda-like ending.

Musical Terms, Signs, and Symbols

Baroque	cantata
fermata	imitation at the fifth
melisma	phrases
ritornello	rhythmic motive ♩♫ ♫
word painting	

Extension

1. The German text has better vowels for singing the melismas than does the English translation. Learn the German text and sing the song in German.
2. Learn the B section from the E. C. Schirmer edition.
3. Listen to the rest of "Cantata No. 78." Find out for which Sunday of the church year Bach wrote it.
4. Find out what was happening in Germany and the rest of the world when Bach wrote this piece.
5. Learn another cantata duet (such as "Duet from Cantata No. 15," edited by Rao and published by Boosey & Hawkes).
6. Examine other Baroque examples of word painting.

Evaluation

Can the singers

- ■ recognize examples of word painting?
- ■ identify imitation when it occurs?
- ■ perform using only the head voice?
- ■ perform lines melodically (without the other part and with appropriate weighting of important syllables)?

Evaluation of the Choral Music Program

The evaluation of educational programs is essential to establishing accountability and credibility of eductional practice among school administrators, boards of education, legislators, and others. Valid data on music programs are especially helpful in justifying the need for quality musical experiences in schools and planning for music program improvements. The Music Educators National Conference, in cooperation with the Educational Testing Service, has taken a leadership role in developing a program evaluation system in music that could bring great benefits to music education in future years.

MENC's program evaluation system, which has items relating directly to vocal and choral music instruction in grades 4–12, includes questions for assessing these music program elements: goals and objectives, leadership, staffing, curriculum and scheduling, instructional materials, equipment, facilities, and student outcomes. Separate questions have been developed for school administrators, music administrators, elementary teachers, middle and junior high school teachers, high school teachers, and students. The program evaluation system has been designed to provide schools and districts maximum flexibility in the use of the instruments to identify and respond to specific school needs. Both objective and subjective data will be made available through use of the questions; both opinions and facts are sought.

A purpose of the evaluation system is to provide diagnostic data that give specific information about areas of music programs that are in need of improvement. Problems related to staffing, curriculum and scheduling, instructional materials, equipment, and facilities are more likely to be resolved when there are valid data to support the claims of teachers and music administrators. Valid data will also provide the kind of information school administrators need to plan for the funding of program improvement. The vocal and choral questions will be especially helpful in compiling data that will be believable and usable by decision makers. It may also be helpful for teachers to create individually developed assessment procedures to substantiate claims they make about music program needs. A goal should be to provide the very best data possible in relation to the accepted standards of a quality music program.

More information about this program evaluation system is available upon request from the Music Educators National Conference.

Glossary

A CAPPELLA	Choral music performed without instrumental accompaniment.
ACCELERANDO	Accelerate the tempo, grow faster.
ACCENT	A musical stress that makes one tone more important than others around it. A dynamic accent is frequently indicated by the sign >.
ACCOMPANIMENT	Any sounds meant to enhance the main melody of a composition by providing a background.
AGNUS DEI	In Roman Catholic rites, the last part of the Ordinary of a Mass.
ALLA BREVE	The time signature ¢ indicating that the tempo should be fast enough so the half note rather than the quarter note receives one beat; $\frac{2}{2}$.
ALTO	The lowest female voice in the vocal range.
ANTHEM	A religious or patriotic song for vocal ensemble, with or without instrumental accompaniment.
ARIA	A song for a solo singer, usually within an opera, an oratorio, or a cantata.
ARRANGEMENT	Adaptation of a composition for instruments or voices that are different from what was originally written.
ART SONG	A solo song composed for performance, as opposed to a folk song.
ATONALITY	Music in which there is no sense of a tonic, or tonal center. Almost all music is tonal. Atonal music was not composed until the twentieth century.
AVANT GARDE	The latest, most recent styles or techniques.
BALLADE	A song or poem that tells a story, usually based on a historical, legendary, or romantic theme.
BALLETT	An English song popular during the Renaissance period. It is dance-like and usually contains a *fa-la* section in the text.
BARITONE	A male voice with a pitch range between a tenor and a bass.
BASS	The lowest part in a musical composition. A male voice with the lowest pitch range.
BEL CANTO	Literally "well sung." Refers to a singing style that emphasizes beautiful tone and brilliant performance rather than the expression of dramatic emotion.
BENEDICTUS	The second part of the Sanctus of the Mass in Roman Catholic services.
BINARY	A musical form that contains only two large contrasting sections (AB form).
BOCCA CHIUSA	Italian for "laughing mouth." Refers to forming a smile with the lips while singing. Singing without words and with the mouth closed is called *bouche fermée*.
BREAK	The voice change between the head vocal register and chest vocal register.
CADENZA	An elaborate solo passage of improvisatory style played or sung by a soloist; frequently played near the end of a composition.
CANON	A polyphonic composition consisting of one or more voices imitating what has already been sounded in one voice and starting at later points in time.

CANTATA	Sacred or secular vocal works consisting of movements for solo voice or a combination of solo voices, instrumental accompaniment, and a chorus.
CANTICLE	A song or hymn using words from the Bible sung in praise of God.
CANTO	A song, melody, chant.
CANTUS FIRMUS	Literally "fixed melody." A melody that is used as the thematic basis for a composition for several voices.
CAROL	Songs of praise, such as the kinds of songs sung at Christmas. The word originally referred to a round dance in celebration of the winter solstice.
CAVATINA	Short solo song, characterized by a simple form, without repetition of words or phrases.
CHAMBER MUSIC	Music intended for a small group of performers.
CHANSON	French for "song."
CHANT	A general term for liturgical music similar to Gregorian plainsong. Also a type of native singing that uses repetitive rhythm and only two or three pitches as in pagan ceremonial music.
CHOIR	Usually refers to a group of singers of various numbers and voicings, or instrumental ensembles of the same family, such as brass choir.
CHORALE	A hymn melody or sacred melody usually harmonized for voices and often sung by a congregation.
CHORD	Two or more pitches sounded simultaneously. A triad is one type of chord.
CHORD PROGRESSION	A series of chords that comprises the harmonic basis of a musical work, phrase, or section.
CHROMATIC	Using pitches from outside the basic key of a composition.
CHURCH MODES	A grouping of pitches that represent the tonal content of a piece of music.

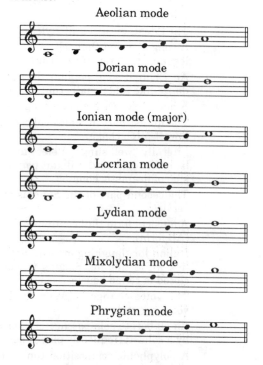

Aeolian mode

Dorian mode

Ionian mode (major)

Locrian mode

Lydian mode

Mixolydian mode

Phrygian mode

COLORATURA	A virtuoso passage consisting of elaborate embellishments and ornamentations, particularly in vocal music; also, the vocalist capable of performing this music.
CONTRALTO	Same as alto voice.
COUNTER SUBJECT/ COUNTER MELODY	A melody of equal or near-equal importance to the primary melody.
DA CAPO	Italian for "from the beginning." A symbol on the musical score that means to return to the beginning and repeat the music to the end or to a place where the term *fine* is written. *Da capo al fine* is abbreviated as *D.C.* or *D.C. al fine.*
DA CAPO ARIA	An elaborate composition for a vocal soloist with instrumental accompaniment, characterized by an ABA form (two sections followed by a repetition of the first section).
DESCANT	An independent melody composed to accompany another melody. A kind of countermelody.
DIATONIC	Pitches that correspond to the notes of a major or minor scale.
DOUBLE CHORUS	Using two choruses in alternation.
DUET	A piece for two equally prominent parts.
EMBELLISHMENT	Same as COLORATURA and ORNAMENTATION.
ENSEMBLE	Any collection of instruments and voices.
EQUAL VOICES	An indication for women's voices only or men's voices only, rather than mixed voices.
FALSETTO	An artificial method of singing using the very high head tones.
FAMILIAR STYLE	A vocal style where the note values and the text syllables move uniformly, as in church hymns.
FOLK SONG	A song of unknown origins in terms of a single composer.
FROTTOLA	Italian secular songs written during the late fifteenth to early sixteenth centuries.
FUGING TUNE	A type of hymn or psalm tune developed during the late eighteenth and early nineteenth centuries in New England.
GENRE	Classifying music by type, according to medium of performance, the purpose of the performance, and the style.
GLORIA	The second item in the Ordinary of the Mass.
GRADUAL	The second item in the Proper of the Mass, a responsorial chant.
GREGORIAN CHANT	The liturgical chant of the Roman Catholic Church, named after Pope Gregory I.
HEMIOLA	Literally, three against two. It most often refers to any rhythm that shifts from a feeling of two to three or from a feeling of three to two. A device often used to compose a ritard by doubling note values.
HOMOPHONY	A texture in which several parts sound at the same time, yet only one part is the principal or leading part.
HYMN	A religious or sacred song.
IMITATION	The act of one part repeating what another part has just sounded.
INTONATION	In performance, relating to singing or playing in tune.
INTROIT	The initial chant of the Proper of the Mass.
KAPELLMEISTER	The director of music, chorus, or orchestra. German.
KYRIE ELEISON	Literally "Lord, have mercy." The first item in the Ordinary of the Mass.
LACRIMOSA	Italian for "mournful." A section of the Requiem Mass.
LAMENTATION	Musical setting of the Lamentations of Jeremiah. The lamentations are sung during specific Roman Catholic services.
LEITMOTIV	A compositional technique of representing characters, situations, or ideas with a musical motif.

LIED/LIEDER	A German song or ballad.
LITANY	Songs of solemn supplications directed to God.
MADRIGAL	A vocal setting of a short lyric poem, popular among art composers in England and Italy during the Renaissance period.
MAGNIFICAT	The canticle of the Virgin. Text is found in the Bible, Luke 1:46–55.
MAJOR SCALE	A scale based on a pattern with whole steps between the first and second, second and third, fourth and fifth, fifth and sixth, sixth and seventh degrees of the scale; and half steps between the third and fourth and the seventh and eighth scale degrees.
MASS	The most solemn service of the Roman Catholic Church celebrating the Eucharist or Last Supper.
MELISMA	An expressive vocal passage where one syllable is sung over several, or many, different pitches.
MESSA-DI-VOCE	An eighteenth-century technique consisting of sustaining a tone while gradually getting louder and then getting softer while singing or playing.
MEZZO SOPRANO	A female voice in the middle range, lower than a soprano but higher than a contralto.
MEZZO VOCE	Singing with a half voice by restraining the volume of tone.
MINOR SCALE	A scale based on a pattern distinguished by the minor third, minor sixth, and minor seventh. Three basic types are found in Tonal music:

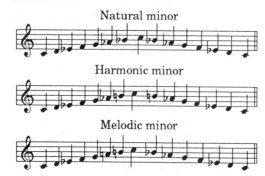

MONODY	Music for solo voice or unison group with an accompaniment.
MONOPHONY	A musical texture consisting of only one actual part, which may be performed by two or more voices or instruments unaccompanied. The oldest type of music.
MOTET	A sacred vocal composition, usually polyphonic and performed without accompaniment.
OFFERTORY	In Roman Catholic liturgy, a hymn, anthem, prayer, or instrumental piece performed during the placement of bread and wine on the altar. The fourth item of the Proper of the Mass.
OFFICE	Services in Roman Catholic liturgy that are distinct from the Mass. They are celebrated eight times a day; the most important Offices in terms of music are Matins, Vespers, Lauds, and Compline.
OPERA	Drama set to music that includes acting, costumes, staging, singing, lighting, and usually an instrumental ensemble.
OPERA BUFFA	An Italian opera or dramatic work with comic elements (buffoons).
OPERETTA	A short opera, often with dialogue between songs.
OPUS	A term used to indicate chronological order of a composition within a composer's output. Latin word meaning "work."

ORATORIO	A composition with a libretto from the Bible or sacred history, performed by solo voices, chorus, and orchestra.
ORDINARY (MASS)	That part of the Roman Catholic liturgy that remains the same regardless of the day in the church year.
OSTINATO	Any pattern—rhythm, chord change, or melody—that is repeated several times to form the accompaniment for another musical pattern.
PART SONG	A choral composition for at least three voices, written in a homophonic style without accompaniment.
PASSION	A large religious work, similar to an ORATORIO, with a text based on the Passion according to one of the four Evangelists.
PENTATONIC SCALE	Any scale that contains only five pitches.
PHRASE	A complete musical statement, usually about four measures long.
PHRASING	The way a phrase is performed to make all tones combine into a unified statement rather than just a collection of successive tones.
PLAINSONG	Monophonic melody that is rhythmically free; often modal. Also, a thirteenth-century name for GREGORIAN CHANT.
POLYCHORAL	A style that divides the choral ensemble into distinct groups that then perform alternately or jointly.
POLYPHONY	A texture in which more than one part can be regarded as melodically important (prominent). Opposite is HOMOPHONY, in which one part is principal and all other parts form an accompaniment.
PORTAMENTO	A singing technique where the voice glides from one pitch to another pitch, rapidly sounding the intermediate tones.
PROPER OF THE MASS	That part of the Roman Catholic liturgy in which parts change, unlike the Ordinary, according to the day and service during which they are performed.
PSALMODY	The musical setting of psalms for singing.
PSALMS	A sacred song or hymn. The psalms are by far the most important texts in Gregorian Chant.
PULSE	The (usually) steady beat that most music projects by its rhythms. The conductor's beat most often outlines the pulse, and we usually tap the pulse when listening to rhythmic music. Same as beat.
QUARTET	A composition for four performers.
QUINTET	A composition for five performers.
RECITATIVE	A singing style that follows the natural inflections of speech. Used in operas and other musical dramatic works to provide information about the characters or the plot.
REGISTER	In the human voice, the level or range of pitch, such as the high or head register, and the low or chest register.
REQUIEM	Composition that sets to music the Mass for the Dead.
RHYTHM PATTERN	Any succession of sounds that forms a distinctive unit.
ROUND	A sung canon in which performers alternately sing the same melody.
ROUNDELAY	A fourteenth-century English adaption of the rondeau form.
SACRED	Referring to music composed for church service.
SANCTUS	The fourth item of the Ordinary of the Mass.
SCALE	Any ordering of successive pitches within an octave; usually used to represent the pitch content of a particular piece of music.
SEA CHANTY	Work songs of English and American sailors.
SECULAR	Referring to music composed for purposes other than for use in church.

SOLFEGGIO	The system of syllables (*do-re-mi-fa-sol-la-ti*) used to help pitch memory. Italian; also solfège (French).
SOLO	A musical passage or whole composition that is sung or played with one performer as the dominating part.
SONG CYCLE	A group of songs based on a common theme, forming a complete musical entity, and performed as a group rather than as separate songs.
SONG FORM	See FORM.
SOPRANO	The highest female voice; the highest voice in a four-part composition.
SOTTO VOCE	Italian for "under the voice," indicating to perform with a soft, subdued sound.
SPIRITUAL	Religious folk songs whose style emanates from the African-American culture.
STROPHIC	A form in which all the verses of the text are sung to the same music.
SUBJECT	A melodic motive or phrase that is the principal theme and the basic factor in the structure of a composition such as a fugue.
SYNCOPATION	A deliberate alteration of the normal beat, pulse, or stress. For instance, placing the stress on the weak beats.
TE DEUM	A song of celebration, thanking and praising God. A hymn rejoicing "Te Deum laudamus" (We praise Thee, O God).
TENOR	The highest natural male voice; in music, the second lowest part in a four-part composition.
TERNARY	Three parts, usually to describe a form in which there are three distinct sections, such as ABA.
TESSITURA	The general location of the majority of pitches for a song.
TEXT	The words that make up a song.
TEXTURE	The way the layers of a musical composition are combined to create its "body."
THROUGH-COMPOSED	A song in which there is different music for each verse or stanza.
TIMBRE	That aspect of sound that defines its quality or color. A clarinet may play the same pitch as a trumpet, but its timbre will be different.
TRANSPOSITION	The act of placing musical tones higher or lower without altering the pattern of relationship of notes.
TREBLE	The highest part of a choral composition, usually the soprano part. Also voices singing in the treble clef.
TRIO	A composition for three parts or voices.
UNISON	The effect of several (two or more) parts singing or playing the same pitches at the same time.
VARIATION	A changed version of a theme or section, varying one or more of the original musical elements.
VERSE	Section of a song sung to different lines of text, usually followed by the chorus.
VERSE-ANTHEM	Choral composition with religious text, performed during services of the Anglican Church.
VESPERS	In the Roman Catholic liturgy, the seventh of the canonical hours of the Office.
VIBRATO	A slight undulation of a pitch that increases the expressive qualities of the tone.
VIRTUOSO	An artist, a great instrumental or vocal performer.
VOICE LEADING	Principles that govern the movement of the various voice parts in compositions.

Bibliography

Note: *While some of these references are no longer in print, copies may still be found in many school, college, university, and public libraries. References out of print at time of publication of this course of study are designated by an asterisk (*).*

Choral References

Ades, Hawley. *Choral Arranging.* Delaware Water Gap, PA: Shawnee Press, 1983.

Alderson, Richard. *Complete Handbook of Voice Training.* West Nyack, NY: Parker Publishing, 1979.

Bartle, Jean Ashworth. *Lifeline for Children's Choir.* London: Oxford University Press, 1988.

Boyd, Jack. *Rehearsal Guide for the Choral Director.* Champaign, IL: Mark Foster Music, 1977.

Christy, Van A. *Foundations in Singing: A Basic Textbook in Vocal Technique and Song Interpretation.* 5th ed. Dubuque, IA: William C. Brown, 1990.

Choral Journal, The. Journal of the American Choral Directors Association. See journal indexes for articles on particular aspects of choral music.

Decker, Harold, and Julius Herford, eds. *Choral Conducting, A Symposium.* 2d ed. New York: Appleton-Century-Crofts, 1988.

Ehmann, Wilhelm, and Frauke Haaseman. *Voice Building for Choirs.* Chapel Hill, NC: Hinshaw Music, 1982.

Ehmann, Wilhelm. *Choral Directing.* Minneapolis: Augsburg, 1968.

Garretson, Robert L. *Conducting Choral Music.* 6th ed. Needham, MA: Allyn and Bacon, 1988.

Green, Elizabeth A. H. *The Modern Conductor.* 3d ed. Englewood Cliffs, NJ: Prentice Hall, 1983.

Heffernan, Charles W. *Choral Music.* Englewood Cliffs, NJ: Prentice Hall, 1982.

*Hillis, Margaret. *At Rehearsals.* New York: American Choral Foundation, 1969.

Howerton, George. *Technique and Style in Choral Singing.* New York: Carl Fischer, 1957.

*Jacobs, Arthur. *Choral Music.* Baltimore: Penguin Books, 1963.

Jipson, Wayne R. *The High School Vocal Music Program.* West Nyack, NY: Parker Publishing, 1972.

Kemp, Helen. *Of Primary Importance.* Dayton, OH: Lorenz Corporation, 1989.

*Krone, Max T. *The Chorus and Its Conductor.* Chicago: Neil Kjos Music, 1945.

Lamb, Gordon H. *Choral Techniques.* 3d ed. Dubuque, IA: William C. Brown, 1988.

*Lamb, Gordon H., ed. *Guide for the Beginning Choral Director.* American Choral Directors Association, 1972.

McRae, Shirley W. *Directing the Children's Choir.* New York: Schirmer Books, 1991.

Marshall, Madeline. *The Singer's Manual of English Diction.* New York: G. Schirmer, 1953.

May, William V., and Craig Tolin. *Pronunciation Guide for Choral Literature.* Reston, VA: Music Educators National Conference, 1987.

*Montani, Nicola A., ed. *Latin Pronunciation According to Roman Usage.* Philadelphia: St. Gregory Guild, 1937.

Music Educators Journal. The principal journal of the Music Educators National Conference. See journal indexes for choral articles.

*Neidig, Kenneth, and John Jennings, eds. *Choral Director's Guide.* West Nyack, NY: Parker
          Publishing, 1967.
*Pooler, Frank, and Brent Pierce. *New Choral Notation (A Handbook).* New York: Walton
          Music, 1971.
  Rao, Doreen. *Choral Music Experience...Education Through Artistry.* Vol 1–5. New York:
          Boosey & Hawkes, 1987.
  Rao, Doreen. *Choral Music for Children.* Reston, VA: Music Educators National Conference,
          1990.
  Rinstad, Eloise. *A Soprano on Her Head.* Moab, UT: Real People Press, 1982.
  Roach, Donald W. *Complete Secondary Choral Music Guide.* West Nyack, NY: Parker
          Publishing, 1989.
  Roe, Paul F. *Choral Music Education.* 2d ed. Englewood Cliffs, NJ: Prentice Hall, 1983.
  Simons, Harriet. *Choral Conducting: A Leadership Teaching Approach.* Champaign, IL:
          Mark Foster Music, 1983.
  Stanton, Royal. *The Dynamic Choral Conductor.* Delaware Water Gap, PA: Shawnee Press,
          1971.
  Swan, Howard. *Conscience of a Profession.* Chapel Hill, NC: Hinshaw Music, 1987.
  Swears, Linda. *Teaching the Elementary School Chorus.* West Nyack, NY: Parker Publishing,
          1985.
  Thomas, Kurt. *The Choral Conductor.* New York: Associated Music Publishers, 1971.
  Ulrich, Homer. *A Survey of Choral Music.* New York: Harcourt Brace Jovanovich, 1973.
*Van Camp, Leonard. *Warm-ups for Minds, Ears, and Voices.* New York: Lawson-Gould, 1973.
  Wilson, Harry Robert. *Artistic Choral Singing.* New York: G. Schirmer, 1959.

General References
  Apel, Willi. *The New Harvard Dictionary of Music.* 2d rev. ed. Edited by Don Randel.
          Cambridge, MA: Harvard University Press, 1986.
  Dart, Thurston. *The Interpretation of Early Music.* Rev. ed. London: Hutchinson University
          Library, 1960.
  Donington, Robert. *The Interpretation of Music.* London: Faber and Faber Limited, 1963.
  Grout, Donald Jay. *A History of Western Music.* 4th ed. New York: W. W. Norton, 1988.
  Hoffer, Charles R. *Teaching Music in the Secondary Schools.* 4th ed. Belmont, CA:
          Wadsworth Publishing, 1991.
*Huls, Helen Steen. *The Adolescent Voice: A Study.* New York: Vantage Press, 1957.
  Kagen, Sergius. *On Studying Singing.* New York: Dover Publications, 1960.
  Lang, Paul Henry. *Music in Western Civilization.* New York: W. W. Norton, 1940.
  McElheran, Brock. *Conducting Techniques: For Beginners and Professionals.* New York:
          Oxford University Press, 1989.
  Rosen, Charles. *The Classical Style: Haydn, Mozart, Beethoven.* New York: W. W. Norton,
          1972.
  Sadie, Stanley ed. *Grove's Dictionary of Music and Musicians.* 5th ed. New York: St. Martin's
          Press, 1980.
  Slonimsky, Nicolas. *Baker's Biographical Dictionary of Musicians.* 7th rev. ed. New York:
          G. Schirmer, 1984.
*Vinquist, Mary, and Neal Zaslow, eds. *Performance Practice: A Bibliography.* New York:
          W. W. Norton, 1971.